Undying Love

The True Story
of a Passion that
Defied Death

Ben Harrison

K&
YP

THE KETCH & YAWL PRESS
MARATHON, FLORIDA

ISBN-13: 978-0-9788949-8-6
ISBN-10: 0-9788949-8-7

The Ketch & Yawl Press, LLC
2315 Overseas Highway
Marathon FL 33050
or
PO Box 5828
Lakeland FL 33807

Visit our Web site at www.ketchandyawl.com
Visit the author's Web site at www.harrison-gallery.com
Cover Design: Lindsay Malboeuf and Tom Corcoran
Cover Photograph: Courtesy of Wright Langley Archives
Autographed Rear Cover Photograph: Elena at age 17

Printed in the United States of America.

0987654321

"I'm about to die ... of love, daroga ... of love.
That's how it is. I ... I loved her so much! And I still love her ... If you knew how beautiful she was when she let me kiss her *alive,* because she'd sworn on her eternal salvation.... Yes, alive, I kissed her alive, and she was as beautiful as a dead woman!"

- GASTON LEROUX
The Phantom of the Opera

Acknowledgments

First, I would like to thank Jean Poulin and Kim Johansen. After hearing me sing several of the songs I had written for the musical play, *Undying Love,* they suggested that I write a book and were very instrumental in the evolution of what you are about to read.

Tom and Lynda Hambright (historians at the Monroe County Library)—in addition to sharing their knowledge of the times and events, went out of their way helping me sift through the "von Cosel" file of aging newspaper clippings and old photographs. Dr. Herman Moore, who for many years wrote an excellent historical column for the *Key West Citizen,* graciously shared a photograph and his knowledge of the episode. Additionally, he helped me get in touch with people here in town who still remember this grave affair.

B.J. Martin and Bill Lorraine were extremely generous for allowing me to see the videos they filmed with townsfolk who personally recalled the Count and Elena. The taped interview with Mrs. Ana Weekley of Fausto's Food Palace, the hometown grocery store that used to be located where Café Marquesa is now, told of some curious purchases the Count made after he built the mausoleum.

Before Rod Bethel passed on, he traded me an autographed copy of his book, *A Halloween Love Story,* for a copy of the words to the song I had written about von Cosel and Elena. It was his copy that I kept constantly by my side and quoted from extensively. I believe he would have enjoyed *Undying Love.* It was kind of Kim McGee, his daughter, to allow us to reproduce one of the photographs from Mr. Bethel's book.

I want to also thank Mrs. Ida Roberts of Roberts Plumbing and her mother Mrs. Grace Rodriguez for telling me about the characters—the way they acted; the way they walked.

The words to "La Boda Negra," "The Black Wedding," the song that played such a major role in the life of von Cosel and the death of Elena were located by local musical historian, the late Joseph Albertson who, before his death, had the largest collection of sheet music filled with songs about the sinking of the *Maine*.

Thanks very much to Kat, who is no longer with us, and Skip MacLeod for allowing the play *Undying Love* to be performed at The Appelrouth Grill. The cast was wonderful: Tom Luna, Vicki Roush, Melody Cooper, Gordon Mackey, the late Mike Alpern, Mira Negron, Armando Lodigiani, Chris Stone, Tom Murtha (the director), Leda and Bruce Seigal (costumes), Quint Lange (drums), Woody Allen (musical director, synthesizer), Rick Worth (set design), Chad Wojnar and Jessica Steele (stage manager and assistant). My appreciation also goes to Robin Deck and John Wells who helped edit the script. Carol Wolff deserves special thanks as does Dan Simpson of Private Ear Recording Studio, where the songs were originally arranged and recorded.

The flavor of the times and those ever-so-interesting tidbits that can be found out only by talking with those who knew first hand what went on were invaluable. Mrs. Juliet Delgado's friendship with Elena enabled me to more accurately describe the tragedy of her untimely death. Mrs. Benildes Remond Sanchez, who worked at the San Carlos Institute, helped me get a better feeling for the Keys in the thirties as did Bascom Grooms—the first person to cross the Overseas Highway on a motorized vehicle (a motor scooter)—Julia Hoffman, Elizabeth Ann Gardner, Louise Parks and G.I. Rodriguez.

Woody Allen, co-author of the music for "Elena's Song," and Din Allen deciphered the Count's Latin phrases. Sean and Laura Koehane shared "The Trial Bay Organ" article written by the Count.

Others who deserve a generous round of applause are: Susan Olsen, Gerry Wood, Judi Bradford and Carol Shaughnessy.

At the Shipwreck Historeum, Michael Alpern and Monica King, gave me the royal treatment. Bob Bender, Creative Services of Key West, scanned and enhanced some of the old photographs.

Both the *Miami Herald* and the *Key West Citizen* were extremely cooperative in allowing us to reprint newspaper articles written at the time. Their reporters did an excellent job of covering the story as it unbelievably unfolded.

I want to thank the late Wright Langley, author and historian, for supplying photographs. The Wright Langley Archives, the Monroe County Library, the *Miami Herald* and Stetson Kennedy, are responsible for preserving the fantastic pictures that tell more than words could ever say. Stetson Kennedy*, who was a friend of the Hoyos family, was also given access to their personal photographs, some of which greatly enrich this story.

Last, but certainly not least, thanks goes out to my mother, the late Mrs. Aleen Caudill, and my wife, Helen, for helping with the editing. Thanks to Ben and Cole for being good kids thus far, and thanks, finally, to Key West for being the exotic place it has been and still is.

*Stetson Kennedy's on-the-scene reportage of the event was published by the magazine *Bohemia of Havana*. A native Floridian, Kennedy lived in Key West during the late 1930's, married a Key West girl (Edith Ogden) and edited *A Guide to Key West* for the WPA Writers' Program (Hastings House, 1941). He is co-author of *South Florida Folklife* (University of Mississippi Press) and other works available from the University Press of Florida and the Pineapple Press. Most recent is *Grits and Grunts: Folkloric Key West*.

Contents

Foreword

I've lived in Key West for 30 years and the exotic, romantic, off-beat aura of the town, its past and its present, never ceases to amaze me. Of the many characters who have walked the patchwork streets lined with sun-bleached wood-framed houses, each different from the other, Count Carl von Cosel was, in my opinion, the strangest and most fascinating of them all.

As a professional guitar player/singer/songwriter, I began composing a song that told of his bizarre love for Elena Hoyos immediately after I read about it in the tourist guide book, *A Key West Companion* by Christopher Cox. My audiences were as amazed as I by the story. My biggest problem was convincing them it was true. Soon, it became the ballad I was most often requested to play, and the subject about which people usually asked when I took a break. That was only the beginning.

I too could not stop thinking of the extraordinary escapades of von Cosel and Elena. After playing the song for about a year, I decided to write a theater musical based upon it:

> *Undying Love*
> *Love from his heart*
> *Not even death*
> *Could keep them apart*

Since what took place was stranger than fiction, I wanted to tell what happened as truthfully as I could. But, piecing things together so I could arrive at "the truth" proved more elusive than I thought it would be. It was like solving a mystery that took place fifty years ago.

Von Cosel's memoirs were the centerpiece of the available information and where I began my research. He wrote them late in life, while sitting in the cramped cockpit of his wingless airplane. The memoirs, which added a complete new dimension to my perceptions, were originally published in a paperback pulp rag called *Fantastic Adventures*. They were later republished in a book titled *A Halloween Love Story* by Rodman Bethel, the son of Otto Bethel, the cemetery sexton at the time of Elena's three burials. On hearing my ballad, Rod gave me a copy.

Next, I began to delve into the newspaper and magazine accounts. When the escapades of Count Carl von Cosel—the title Carl Tanzler swore was his—came to light in 1940, they were covered extensively by newspapers all over the country because the tale had an almost supernatural aura, and was a welcome break from the grim news emanating from Europe and the impending Second World War—Hitler and Nazi Germany. The newspapers likened von Cosel to Don Quixote, the hopeless romantic tilting with the windmill of death; and El Cid, the Spanish conquistador whose corpse was put upon his horse to terrify the enemy.

Soon I turned to the recollections of people who were here when the events took place. These helped bring the story to life.

One Cuban gentleman I spoke with told me that Elena Hoyos often had a red rose in her hair and that her beauty was so unusual that tourists often took pictures of her because she was so striking.

Bienvenido Perez, the Chief of Police, who helped bury Elena for the final time, knew her well because, as a young man, he fancied Elena's cousin, Florinda. "Hers was a delicate, Spanish-Cuban type beauty. Her fair and blemishless skin seemed to glow with an inner light. Her dark brown eyes were vivacious and flashed fire. But Elena was not the stormy, volatile, imperious Latin type. Rather, she was softly feminine and infinitely kind."

In one of my conversations with Mrs. Roberts at Roberts Plumbing, I found out that when she was a little girl, along with everyone else, she viewed Elena's body after it had been taken from von Cosel's house. Her mother, Mrs. Grace Rodriguez, knew Elena. She lived around the corner, and they conversed regularly. It was Mrs. Rodriguez who told me how von Cosel strutted erectly with his cane as he walked about town, and it was she who confirmed an allegation von Cosel made in his memoirs: Louis, the no-good dirty rat who was Elena's husband, left her for another woman.

I met Tom Hambright, the Monroe County Library historian and some of the old timers who frequent his section of the library. The more I learned, the more there was to find out. The answer to one question unearthed other questions. Everyone I have talked to who was alive at the time of the viewing of Elena's body has a different story or perspective on the characters.

At the same time I was researching, I was working on the decks of a thirty-eight foot sailboat. It was mindless work in the sun-drenched heat of summer that allowed me to think. Each day as I fitted and refurbished the wood under the summer sun, I chose a different character and tried to look at the quirky events through his eyes, envisioning how I would react if I were him ... or her.

I could take only three or four hours of deck work a day; afterwards, I came home and strapped my youngest son, who was a baby at the time, into a back-pack. With me thinking and Cole along for the ride, we roamed all over town.

We walked through the development now called the Truman Annex and studied the building that used to be the Marine Hospital. Standing there (with small hands on my head) I could visualize Elena on the balcony, her raven black ringlets blowing in the wind as her sad dark eyes gazed at the hypnotizing flow of water charging in and out of the harbor as the tides came and went. I could see a euphoric von Cosel marveling at the beauty of the sky, the glaring white sand as it met the greenish-blue sea and the gulls circling overhead on the mornings he entered his mole-like X-ray laboratory.

Finally, I finished my work on the boat so I could complete the play. It was performed by some of the best actors and musicians in town to overflowing crowds at a small bar on Appelrouth Lane. Yet, instead of moving on, I could not let the story go. It·was music, one song in particular, that pushed von Cosel over the edge; and it was a song, in a convoluted way, that prompted me to write this book.

As I learned more and more about the personalities of the characters, tried to separate fact from myth, and untangle the thread of this gothic tale of obsessive love and melancholy madness, I imagined their thoughts and heard their voices in my head. An unexpected and eerie feeling of their presence followed me. It remained with me as I wrote.

This is the fourth printing of *Undying Love* since it was originally published in 1997. Though I since have had the pleasure of speaking with numerous people familiar with this unusual piece of Key West history, no new significant information has come to my attention that would cause me to revise or augment the original version.

The personalities, events, actions, and conversations portrayed within the story have been reconstructed from extensive interviews and research, utilizing court documents, letters, personal papers, press accounts, and the memories of participants.

As best I can discern, this is what truly took place.

Prologue

It was a mystical night for Count Carl von Cosel. He double-checked everything before taking the wagon, blanket, cushions, and rope down the stairs into the mausoleum. A black crucifix above Elena Hoyos's coffin inexplicably glowed with a soft light as the Count extracted the inner casket from the outer one. With difficulty because the caskets were heavy, von Cosel pushed, shoved, pulled, and maneuvered the inner one onto the grass outside of the tomb, closed and locked the tomb door.

> I was prepared to risk my life, and to face any danger which would cross my path this night. There was no half way, this was clear to me. Once it was started, it had to be carried out to a finish…. This was my resolve. Besides, I did not know of a single person whom I could ask for help. Not a single human being I could trust who would be reliably discreet. And she would have to come out, if ever I was to take proper care of her.

He then loaded his Elena onto the little wagon with rubber cushions on either end. The blanket with the crucifix on top was tied around the casket with the rope. Their remarkable journey had begun.

Count von Cosel, in his memoirs written in Zephyrhills, Florida, after he left Key West (highlighted in bold throughout this book), describes the extraordinary night:

> A wonderfully elated feeling took complete possession of my entire being, as though a second spirit had entered my soul. It seemed that a bodyguard of veiled angels had formed

on both sides and were coming along with us and a great inspiration filled me then. It made me feel like a victor, holding the triumphal entry in a world forgotten and buried. I felt secure, protected, and invulnerable. No matter what was coming against us now, nothing could harm either one of us any more.

There was no place for the living here on this blackest of nights.

All of the cemetery was alive with souls which came out of the graves from all sides, moving and thronging all around us. It was indeed like a festival among the departed, as they moved up on all sides. It was like a great divine wedding march for me, taking place. It could not be a funeral march, for all seemed happy and joyful and interested in silent admiration watching as the white forms of angels filed past with Elena and me in their midst. They were everywhere, none blocking our way, but all of them melting out of our way. It seemed as if they had never seen such a celebration in this cemetery before. It was as if all were delighted and desirous to help us. The little cart, for all its weight, seemed almost to run by itself. It responded to the slightest touch of my hand, which gave me the impression of being aided on by friendly hands, reaching out of the ground.

Von Cosel's spirit soared until disaster struck. As he struggled to lift the coffin over the cemetery fence, the ground collapsed and the whole load fell. A foul liquid started dripping on his finest clothes.

With super-human effort, he was able to get the casket to the little shed he had rented as a halfway house. He closed the leaky casket valve and took off all of his clothes. Since there was no running water nearby, he had to wash himself and his clothes with a bottle of whiskey he found on a shelf.

Still smelling strong, but more like liquor now, I closed up the house and went home by a long round about way, so as to give the wind and air a chance to take away the odor and dry my clothes.

Stoically, Count Carl von Cosel walked the dark streets of Key

West in his soiled wedding tuxedo, wearing his crushed new felt fedora, trying to figure out how to get into the room he had rented from Elena's parents without waking anyone. Once inside, he snuck into the bathroom and proceeded to scrub his skin vigorously.

The following day, he left the coffin "at rest."

But, the day after, seemingly driven—"promises to the dead are sacred"—he took Elena from the halfway house and loaded her into a large sedan.

Everything went fine; I arrived at the hospital grounds where the plane was without incident. This part of the hospital grounds, being behind the morgue, was quite deserted evenings. Undisturbed, I had now moved my beloved into the cabin of the plane. She now had taken full possession of it.

"Come fly with me and be my wife, my heart thy resting place will be." An old German song Carl's mother used to sing to him played over and over in his mind as he stood back and looked at his wonderful airship which now held his wonderful bride. With the sea sparkling in the background and the blue sky above, Carl von Cosel put his hands together and pulled them to his chest.

There was so much more that had to be done....

Chapter One
Stranger Than Fiction

In 1926 Karl Tanzler left Germany, a country that was dispirited and defeated after the First World War, and sailed across the Atlantic Ocean to the United States, the victorious country that would become his new home. Leaving his young wife, Doris, and two daughters behind, he was coming to join his sister in Zephyrhills, Florida, and begin a new life. The plan was for his family to follow once he had settled and felt he could provide for them. Because his destination was Florida, he chose to sail on the Holland-American liner, *Edam,* on February 6, 1926, from Rotterdam bound for Cuba. Tanzler would then make the ninety-mile sea voyage to Key West and his final four hundred miles northward over land.

If, at that time, someone had told Mr. Tanzler that he would, in the near future, forsake his legal, real-life wife and steal a dead woman from her crypt, he probably would have thought they were crazy.

Yet, his memoirs reveal that, upon disembarking in Cuba for a brief stay before boarding the ferry that brought him to his final destination, Cayo Hueso (Island of Bones, the name the Spanish gave the island before it became Key West), Tanzler already was fashioning a new identity, comparing himself to Ulysses.

> I, being a bachelor, set out on an Odyssey....
> It was the time of the carnival and all of Havana seemed to be intoxicated with the carnival spirit. I had never seen anything like it; originally my plans had been to take the ferry to Key West the very next morning. As it was I stayed four days, not to amuse myself but held to the spot by some strange, irrational hope that I could find my lost bride in this carnival crowd.

This was probably because there were so many beautiful ladies of the Spanish type who somehow resembled her, and because in this carnival time so many of them wore veils, and fairylike dresses which made the similarity still more possible. As if I were Spanish or a South American gentleman myself, I spent many hours on the promenade where the band played against the thunder of the surf and against the mad rush of the big, open cars in which the Beauty Queens of Havana came sailing by, in an endless procession.... But, looking everywhere and always expectant of midnight when the veils of all those beautiful girls fell, I never met with my loved one....

On March 1, 1926, I made up my mind that she was not among the ladies of the Carnival and that I would seek my relatives in Florida ... drawn by some mysterious force....

Karl's first impression of Key West wasn't a particularly favorable one. The terrain was, he thought, less beautiful than the mountains of Cuba. But in Cuba he had not found his dream love and so his search continued. The Key West he saw upon arrival was not terribly different looking than "Old Town" is today. There are more tourists now and the prices have escalated, but the houses are the same ones that were built near the end of the eighteen hundreds and early nineteen hundreds from sturdy "heart" pine that has survived hurricanes, progress, and even the destructive, tenacious wood-chomping termites.

Built by shipwrights, the homes were in the purest sense handcrafted. Though there was electricity as early as 1903, power tools were non-existent. Sawing and shaping were done with hand tools, and pegs were often used in place of bolts or nails for fastening structural beams together. There was an unwritten code among builders that they wouldn't build look-alike structures. Few used plans as most were drawn in the dirt and structurally engineered in the minds of the carpenters.

The Key West that Karl Tanzler saw after he got off the ferry occupied roughly two miles by two miles—about four square miles. Why the wood frame homes, some one story, some two, were built so close together has been attributed to several factors: first, everyone wanted to be close to the waterfront because that was where day-to-day commerce took place. In fact, the homes of the sea captains often had "widow's walks" perched on their roofs, not for the widows, but to enable the owner to look seaward and check out the action in the harbor. With a spy glass they could see if there were any ships that had wrecked on the reef.

In addition to the proximity to the waterfront, it was believed the close-knit homes would shelter each other in a violent storm. Another reason for the closeness was the cigar industry that flourished for a while. Housing was needed for the employees; so the owners built numerous small inexpensive homes that were literally only a few feet apart because land was, even then, at a premium.

Because a telegram had failed to reach his relatives, there was no one to greet Karl Tanzler when he disembarked from his ship and cleared customs at the red brick Custom House overlooking the harbor, next to the Navy base. Since the last train out had departed, he was left there feeling lonely and out of place in a strange land. Karl briefly surveyed the town before deciding to walk along the railroad tracks under a full moon that made the tropical night only slightly darker than the day.

In the morning, twelve miles from Key West, carrying the few possessions he had brought with him from the old world, Karl climbed aboard the Overseas Railroad and rode the rest of the way to Miami. From there he traveled north to the small town of Zephyrhills, close to Tampa and St. Petersburg, to join his sister and begin a new life.

Once there, he sent a congratulatory watercolor that he had painted to his wife waiting in Dresden. Handwritten on the back, in German, was "Happy Birthday, 7 September 1926. It's a different world in Florida."

When Karl's wife and children arrived in 1927, their reunion was brief. It may have been no more than a domestic argument, but whatever happened, Karl Tanzler walked out and left them there while he followed his ethereal dreams.

No doubt they were ill suited for each other. Doris Tanzler, half Karl Tanzler's age, was stocky, healthy, determined, and practical. Strong-willed, she insisted once she was in America that her daughters speak only English and learn the ways of the people in their adopted country. On the other hand, Karl Tanzler, fifty years old, was an imaginative, impractical inventor, scientist, electrical wizard, and sometimes ingenious liar. He'd already begun to mix fact and fantasy in the search for his dream lover. Later, in his memoirs he wrote that when he arrived in Havana he was a bachelor, Ulysses in search of Elena. In reality he was a husband with a family.

During his first years in Florida, Tanzler "Americanized" his first name by spelling it Carl rather than Karl. He also bought some land on which he laid the foundation for a home.

> The Florida boom, however, was quickly followed by a crash and it became necessary for me to earn a living as a specialist. The Marine Hospital at Key West employed me as a pathologist and X-ray specialist; I built up a fairly well equipped X-ray department and peace of mind in scientific work until that fateful day of April 22, 1930.

A woman who worked with him at the hospital described von Cosel as destitute. Willing to take any job in the beginning, he was an attendant who cleaned up after procedures. Yet he must have had some medical knowledge as it didn't take long for him to persuade his superiors, especially Dr. Lombard who was the head of the hospital, that he was a technician capable of operating the X-ray apparatus.

Two articles that appeared in the *Key West Citizen* that "fateful" year of 1930 add information about the place von Cosel worked. One was a response to accusations made in the *Miami News* describing the Marine Hospital as nothing other than a saloon and brothel—charges that were angrily denied by the doctors and the staff. The other stated that "Patients at Marine Hospital Will Have Christmas Second to None in Whole Island City." The final sentence in the article was, "Technician Carl Tanzler cooperated by helping with the decorations."

The immoral behavior charges were ludicrous. However, the use of medicinal alcohol was liberal during the strained years of Prohibition. The truth was all of southern Florida was remiss in rooting out the vice surrounding them: horse racing, jazz, gambling, booze, and easy women were all part of the sand, sun, and fun image Henry Flagler and others were promoting to attract tourists.

Key West was every bit as sinful as the mainland, but in a different way. Though a train came to the island, it was still one-hundred and fifty miles from Miami and considered out-of-the-way. By automobile, it was a long trip because ferries had to be taken over the large spans of water.

Isolated from mainstream America, Key West developed early-on its own personality and ethics. Articles of this era written about the town often begin with a statement something like this: "Key West, the tropical paradise known for its live and let live attitude." Individuals felt free to choose the kind of life they wanted to live.

In 1930, if you wanted to be a smuggler, you were in good company because Cuban rum was flowing like a river over the Florida Straits, on its way to gangsters in charge of distribution. If you were a writer or artist, Ernest Hemingway and others had placed their stamp of approval on the creative atmosphere. This was the period Hemingway roamed the streets of Key West, drank at Sloppy Joe's and wrote *To Have and Have Not,* and "The Snows of Kilimanjaro." If you wanted to be a lawyer, there were ample defendants. People certainly didn't want their daughters to become prostitutes, yet "sporting houses" operated openly.

Surrounded by the Atlantic Ocean and the Gulf of Mexico, the ambivalent, casual way locals have failed to respect certain laws came directly from being a seafaring community which has always had a law and code of behavior all of its own, even more so then than now. Piracy, treasure hunting, and wrecking were a way of life in Key West during the mid-eighteen hundreds—rough and tumble, hell or high water was the moral compass of the island inhabitants.

These sea captains were tough as "iron" wood, as were their transient crews. For any sailor having trouble with the law, as many did, Key West was a good place to get lost and make a little money. Inevitably, wild men with a lot of jingle in their pockets were a magnet for wild women with whom they could share, among other things, bottles of Caribbean rum and Cuban cigars.

"Wrecking" was essentially a maritime way to legally claim ownership (salvage the cargo or loot the ship, depending on the participants' point of view) of ships that wrecked on the reef. For a sailing ship, the Straits of Florida were extremely treacherous waters. The Gulf Stream coupled with the swift north and south tidal currents from the Gulf of Mexico made passage difficult for the ships that, without motors, depended on the wind. Blasting through the narrows at four or five knots, the Gulf Stream goes from west to east. The prevailing wind blows from east to west. When the wind and the current are from opposite directions, the wave actions are at odds with each other and, even in light air, abnormally high and steep.

A sailing ship was usually going with the wind or with the opposing current in the churning ocean saturated with dolphin, kingfish, sailfish, marlin, and dorado—unless it was winter and the northers were blowing forty knots or there was a hurricane in the vicinity. Navigating the relatively narrow straits at night was a vexatious undertaking for a ship powered by the wind.

If the wrecking business got slow, navigational lights were changed to confuse the captain in hopes he would make a mistake and run aground. It was so lucrative an enterprise that the booty from these wrecks made Key West the richest city per capita in the United States. Many of the delicately detailed dresses worn by local girls were originally destined for someone else, and more than one silver service was inscribed with initials that differed from the family using it. Homes were richly decorated with expensive burl-topped walnut, cherry, or mahogany furniture bound for New Orleans, Louisiana, located at the mouth of the Mississippi River.

In 1856, before the Civil War, the horizon was dotted daily with the white sails of as many as a hundred square riggers with finished products on their way to ports along the Gulf of Mexico or returning to the eastern seaboard with cotton and other raw materials.

The local favorite story is about a preacher who was a wrecker on the side, or vice versa. From the pulpit he could see what the congregation could not, a compatriot signaling that there was a wreck. That Sunday, seizing the moment without missing a beat, he quickly strode down the aisle continuing his sermon in a booming voice. Quoting from Corinthians about the great race man should carry on in pursuit of salvation—he took off out the door, running toward his boat, getting a jump on the congregation.

"Wreck Ashore!" was the cry that had everyone scrambling to the docks and casting off the dock lines. The first to the wreck had the salvage rights so the races to the reef were cut-throat competitions with each captain and crew pushing his schooner to the limit. Because foul weather was usually the culprit, the daring and ruggedness of the wreckers was legendary.

Averaging a wreck a week, the bounty was enormous. When a

cargo of pianos was salvaged, the wrecker gratuitously gave one, free of charge, to each home in Key West which prompted, it's been said, a much greater local appreciation of music. Like drug money, there was plenty of everything to go around in those untamed prosperous days. Luxury items were like picking key limes from the, albeit, thorny tree.

The other most frequently used descriptive adjective is "laid-back." If ever there was a time in Key's history when it was laid-back, the decade Count con Cosel happened to live here was the one. Nationally, the Great Depression was a sad encore for the Roaring Twenties. Formerly successful New York businessmen jumped out of buildings. Formerly hardworking Midwesterners starved and froze while searching for a way to survive in a cruel world.

Key West, due to its location and the ingenuity of its residents, had a somewhat easier time. Roosevelt's New Deal brought W.P.A. (Work Projects Administration) make-work jobs which paid the workers enough money to buy a few luxuries like sugar and flour. Even so, most of the town was unemployed. Paradoxically, this time period brings a twinkle to the eyes of the old-timers I've talked to about the good-old-days, when Carl von Cosel and the love of his life, Elena, lived in their town.

The good news was, though there wasn't much work, no one froze. There was plenty of shelter—homes and rooms to go around. The windows of the wood-frame, Bahamian/New England style houses were open to the sea breeze. A hand-held fan would keep a person comfortable in the afternoon before the sun went down and the cool of the evening replaced the heat of the day.

There was food and there was drink. The abundance of seafood surrounding the wildly colored coral reef far exceeded what was required to feed everyone well—lobster, conch, yellowtail, grits, and grunts (a small, tasty fish that was easily caught from piers). And, there were chickens, lots of chickens. In addition to enriching their food supply, cock-fighting was a continuing part of the Key West-Cuban culture.

If someone could afford a mid-day or an after-dinner cigar, Key West had plenty of cigar makers. In fact, according to Count von Cosel, Elena's father was a cigar maker who immigrated to Key West from Cuba when owners re-located their cigar factories here—

before they moved them to Tampa. At one time there were one hundred and sixteen different cigar brands in Key West, including one named "La Elena."

During the Depression, a cigar maker might trade a few cigars for a mangrove snapper or some rum. Bartering and sharing was how people got along. There were only about eleven or twelve thousand people on the island then. Everyone knew everyone. Everything was within walking distance. At night, sitting on the porch listening to Spanish music broadcast from station CMQ in Havana, conversation, laughter, and friendship came easily.

As fate would have it, it was the romantic Spanish song, "La Boda Negra" (The Black Wedding) often heard on the radio, that would play a major role in the bizarre events that would eventually unfold between the German immigrant Carl von Cosel and Elena Hoyos. According to friends, it was one of Elena's favorites.

Though most people here in Key West believe the song was written about our strange hero von Cosel and his unwitting heroine, Elena, it certainly was the other way around. Although pinning down the specific date the song was written by Colombian romanticist Alberto Villalon has proven difficult (probably the late 1800s), it was popular in Cuba during the twenties and early thirties. In 1936, it was included on a recorded collection of favorite Mexican Folk songs by the legendary Tex/Mex folk singer, Lydia Mendosa.

Despite being written decades earlier, the song's story almost chillingly foreshadows that of von Cosel's and Elena:

> *You must listen to a story I was told*
> *By an undertaker of the region*
> *A young man's lover died before their wedding*
> *Without her love he simply could not reason*
>
> *At night he would visit the graveyard*
> *And think about the days she was alive*
> *His tears would fall upon her tombstone*
> *The tombstone of the girl to be his bride*
>
> *On a night when thunder roared and lightning flashed*
> *He broke apart the tombstone of her grave*
> *And with his hands he dug into the earth*

And in his arms he carried her away

By a flickering funeral candle light
On his bed that flowers covered
He gently lay the body of his sweetheart
And said his wedding vows to his dead lover

On her head he placed a wreath of flowers
Full of love he held her close to him
He closed his eyes as he gently kissed her
Never again would he awaken

Llevo la novia al talamo mullido
Junto a ella se acosto enamorado
Para siempre se quedo dormido
Al esquelto regido abrasado

The last line literally translates, "her rigid skeleton he embraced," and in Spanish the words suggest the young man committed suicide after reciting the wedding vows. For Count von Cosel the serenade had a special meaning.

Ever since the moon began to wane, Elena had begun to sing in her casket with a very soft, clear voice which became just a little bit stronger from night to night. It was always the same old Spanish song about a lover who opens the grave of his dead bride. I could distinctly hear and understand its every word.

This always lasted for no longer than perhaps ten minutes and then she fell silent as if expecting me to speak.

"Darling," I would say, "very soon now the moon will change, the hour approaches when I shall take you home with me. I will clean you and wash you and I will put on your bridal dress, with veil and crown and all. Thus, as my bride, you will stay with me forever."

Chapter Two
Elena Milagro Hoyos

E lena Milagro Hoyos Mesa was named in the traditional Hispanic manner. Hoyos was the name she took from her father; Milagro came from her mother; and Mesa she took from her husband when they were married.

Of her sisters, Florinda was the eldest, Celia, the youngest, and Elena, the middle daughter born. All three grew up in Key West, and there is nothing to indicate that Elena's childhood was anything other than normal. Supposedly, her family was well-to-do in Cuba before falling on hard times and moving to Key West to work in the cigar factories. Cubans are known for their love of family, and if you were a fellow Cuban you were treated like a relative. The chaotic Hoyos household was no exception. Uncles, cousins, aunts cooking; boyfriends, girlfriends, and children constantly coming and going; loud conversation, laughter, and tears were all a part of her upbringing.

As youngsters they went to school, played, and looked forward to the Saturday matinee at The Strand movie theater with its ornate, brightly painted façade. For five cents they could pass through the fancy tiled foyer and swoon at Rudolph Valentino or laugh at Charlie Chaplin.

Singing, and especially dancing, were two things all three girls did well. Attending the dances held at the Cuban Club on Duval, they were popular and sought-after dance partners. The hot dances at the time were the rhumba, the samba, the cha-cha, a two-step called Tony's Wife, and the always festive conga line.

In a photograph of Elena posing with another girl and two young men in front of the Athletic Club, another dance spot, she looks like a cute, trim but developing thirteen- or fourteen-year-old. In the background, up on the front porch, men can be seen wearing fashionably dandy, vaudeville flat-top hats.

The Hoyos's home was located on Watson Street, one street over from White Street, near the intersection of what is now called Truman Avenue. Then it was officially called Rocky Road until it was paved and re-named Division Street. Horse-drawn trolleys and then electrical trolleys went up and down the rails in the middle of both White Street and Division, which were originally paved with reddish-brown brick. In fact, the intersection of White and Division was known as "Transfer Corner," where the trolleys turned around using Varela and Virginia Streets. Until the trolleys were powered by electricity, it wasn't much faster than walking, but for a few pennies, one could ride to and from downtown and Duval Street, which was the town's main street and the center of commerce.

Most of the single-story homes in the area where Elena lived were built around the turn of the century by tobacco barrons to house the cigar makers. Daily, both men and women filed into one of the large brick buildings where they sat in straight-backed chairs in front of a wooden tray carved to aid them in hand rolling the leaves. Quaintly, in the middle of the warehouse-like workplace, elevated on a small platform surround by a railing, "readers" with powerfully resonant voices read stories to relieve the monotony of making one cigar after another.

One thing the people who knew her agree upon—Elena Hoyos, with raven black ringlets of silky hair falling around her shoulders, was very beautiful and the most giving of the three sisters. Mrs. Juliet Delgado, a close friend of Elena's, recalled how exuberant and "full of life" she was. Elena's family, like many others, had fallen on hard times. When Miss Juliet became Mrs. Delgado, Elena could only afford to give her a hand-stitched garter for the occasion. "We were so poor back then that we had to make mascara from Vaseline and the charcoal of burnt matches. Dampened red crepe paper was rubbed on our cheeks for rouge, and red cake coloring was the closest thing we had to lipstick." Fifty cents would buy a cotton print dress made by Mrs. Delgado's mother, a seamstress. Leather sandals for festive occasions were a coveted luxury.

A photograph of Elena that eventually appeared in the newspapers showed her in her middle teens dressed in the "flapper" style, popular in the twenties. Wearing her sparkling necklace, gold earrings, and filmy scarf with a big bow on the side, she looked ready to dance the night away on the hardwood floors at the Cuban Club. Perhaps she was going to meet her fiancé, Luis Mesa, the evening the photographer made her stand motionless in front of his camera.

Another beguiling picture taken of Elena after her engagement but before the wedding, shows her sensuous lips slightly parted in a half smile exposing perfect, white teeth. She looks the essence of glamour. Stunning, confident, ravishingly more mature, a red rose was pinned to her white fringed dress between her bosom in addition to the one she customarily wore in her hair over her left ear. Her good looks and lovely singing voice made her a popular performer in several special events held at the San Carlos Theater.

In a third photograph, Elena is a blushing, comely eighteen-year-old bride, smiling radiantly as she stands next to her husband on the day of their wedding. Luis, handsome with a mischievous smile on his face, seems equally overjoyed. Life must have seemed sweet as Señorita Hoyos took the bridal walk down the aisle in her exquisite white lace gown on February 18, 1926—the same month and year that Karl Tanzler set sail for Florida.

Luis and Elena's courtship, the wedding, and the subsequent months of bliss were her happiest. Making love with the passion of newlyweds, it came as no surprise that she was pregnant not many months after the marriage ceremony.

It must have perplexed her that a future seemingly so bright and filled with promise could dim so quickly. First, her pregnancy ended tragically on November 5, when she suffered a miscarriage.

Her parents and those around her then thought when she began looking wan, that the poor condition was due to grieving over the loss of the child.

However, as Elena's health deteriorated, her family realized the cause had to be physical and not the effects of sorrow. There was but one thing to do and that was to see the family physician. The recurring cough she developed was heart-breaking because numerous cases of tuberculosis had been diagnosed at the Marine Hospital and the word had spread around town.

In the early stages of the disease, the symptoms of adult pulmonary tuberculosis aren't usually apparent until the disease advances to the point where lesions appear on X-ray. Its onset is usually insidious—fever, malaise, and weight loss. At first the cough is dry and occurs only in the morning. Without up-to-date treatment, the cough becomes more pronounced and painful until the infected wastes away.

Today, tuberculosis, rarely fatal though still serious, is treated with several drugs including chemotherapy. But, at the time of Elena's illness, it was untreatable because medical knowledge had not advanced sufficiently to do much other than diagnose the disease. In Key West during the thirties, it was the number one cause of death, especially among cigar factory workers who passed the germs from one to another in the close confines of their workplace. Of the various strains of tuberculosis, the most dangerous form and the kind Elena Hoyos had, was the type called "hasty consumption," because it quickly consumed those unfortunate enough to contract it. Realizing the seriousness of the situation, her doctor immediately referred her to the Naval Marine Hospital for a blood test and an X-ray.

It was at the time a medium sized, three-story facility and the only one for miles around. For that reason, it was open to the public in general, not just the military. Overlooking the deep water channel, the harbor, and the uninhabited keys to the west, the view from the hospital balcony of the pristine sea meeting the blue sky was picturesque.

Commander Lombard, the physician in charge, had been transferred from New Orleans where he had, with some success, battled the Bubonic Plague. A hospital worker who was there at the time described him as a kind, understanding, and sympathetic man who, along with his wife, raised two fine children. Tolerant and open-minded should be added to the list of qualities she used to describe him. It was under his stewardship that Carl Tanzler was hired and rose to the position he had when Elena came to the hospital for treatment.

Dreading the hospital visit, fearing the results, Elena and her husband, Luis, together rode the trolley and then walked the remaining blocks to the hospital for the appointment. Once there, he stayed outside in the waiting room while she was ushered into an examining room where a distinguished looking gentleman with an imperial beard and mustache prepared to take the blood sample from Elena.

Although there is no record of Elena's first impression of von Cosel, he described his intense immediate reaction to her:

In the middle of my routine work, I received a call from the head office to go and take a blood test from a young señorita who, as an outpatient, had come for examination. I hardly looked at the patient as I entered the room. The first thing I noticed of her personality as I bent down to take a drop of blood from one of her fingertips, rather than one of her ears which were too exquisitely lovely to mar, was that her hand was unusually small: its long tapering fingers the loveliest I had ever seen. As the needle struck, the hand twitched a little and it was then that from my kneeling position, I raised my head for the first time to say,

"I'm very sorry to have caused you pain; forgive me please."

Her face had been hidden by her hand, so that I had hardly seen it as I first entered the room. But now she withdrew her hand to answer me and I looked into a face of unearthly beauty, the face of the bride which had been promised to me by my ancestor forty years before.

I was so thunderstruck, I hardly heard her saying:

"It didn't hurt much. Excuse my nervousness."

Her voice was soft and sweet and childlike. It reminded me of a mockingbird's song in spring. She spoke with a Spanish accent, yet her English was cultured and quite good.

Having performed the duty for which I had been called, I had no excuse to stay any longer in the room. Feeling very shaky, I arose and, much too confused to say anything, I merely bowed myself out, not knowing whether I was walking or dreaming.

Elena had no idea of von Cosel's attraction to her on that windy afternoon, nor had she any idea what fate had in store for her.

But von Cosel could not stop thinking of the beautiful young woman who he felt certain was the bride he had for so long been seeking.

Back in my lab I sat for a while.... Yes it was she whom at last I found in the flesh, and for proof that she really was alive I held in hand the little glass tube with a drop of her red blood. A nurse brought me the record sheet for me to enter the results of my test.

There was nothing much the matter with her blood but it gave me a shock to read on the top of the record sheet the "Mrs." before the name of Elena Hoyos. So she belonged to somebody else. Was there a curse upon me that after this search of four decades had come to an end, I should lose her again at the very moment I had finally discovered her, my promised bride?

Even so I felt indescribably happy. What, after all, did it matter if she belonged to another; hadn't I also belonged to another years ago? Over all these years, what was there in a husband's name or even in a husband's existence? All this had very little to do with me and Elena. The main thing was that I found her and that she was ill and that I was best qualified and in a position to help her.

Legally, Carl Tanzler still belonged to another who was caring for their children, but on meeting Elena, something fractured because, after this, von Cosel mentally turned his familial responsibilities off as one might turn off a water faucet. Thereafter he rarely thought of wife and children, and his memoirs reflect his lack of concern for their welfare. "I also belonged to another years ago," is the only mention in his memoirs of the wife he had married and the offspring he had sired.

He had now fallen completely, desperately in love with Elena.

Who knows what causes a person to fall desperately, head-over-heels in love? A reporter for the *Miami Herald* described von Cosel's obsession this way: "The scientist, apparently sane in all activities, will be regarded as somewhat 'teched in the head' in this particular romance. But then romance, as we all agree, does perform mysterious tricks on the mind, and even the most level-headed man may fall victim to this craze that has kept the world in a dither since the beginning of time."

To add to Elena's misfortunes—losing a child and learning she was seriously ill—her husband, Luis, abandoned her for another woman and left Key West for Tampa and eventually Miami, where he became a waiter in a restaurant on Calle Ocho, Eighth Street. Though he claimed Elena's illness had nothing to do with their failed marriage, realistically it forced him to make a difficult choice—stay and perhaps die of a highly contagious form of tuberculosis or leave and live to love again. Elena was a walking infectious time-bomb with a disease that would later claim the entire Hoyos family—mother, father, older and younger sisters. Only one person, Count Carl von Cosel, was jubilant when he learned of the break-up:

Elena and her husband had separated, as he had been responsible for her suffering. It was probably only human that this fact filled my heart with joy. Also it filled me with deep pity when tears welled up in the beautiful eyes of my Elena and she pointed to a car as it passed by the house.

"There he goes, he who was my husband. He now lives with another girl."

Impulsively, I took her hand between mine and said, "Don't worry over it, and don't worry about anything any more, from now on I am going to take care of you." She thanked me with a happy little smile and like a child, she said: "Yes, doctor, I'm sure you will."

Chapter Three

Count Carl von Cosel

C ount Carl von Cosel's walk wasn't really a walk; it was more of a swagger. As for the theatrical way he carried his silver-tipped cane (or umbrella if it was the rainy season) it was obvious to anyone who observed him that the Count felt superior.

"Ct. Carl Tanzler von Cosel" was the way he signed his name on a handwritten letter mailed from Zephyrhills, Florida, late in life. The "a" in Tanzler was pronounced like the "a" in "father." While he lived in Key West, however, he always referred to himself as Count Carl von Cosel. Virtually every newspaper article referred to him as Karl von Cosel with a "K"; however, in the handwritten letter he signs off as, "Ct. Carl" with a "C" because it was more American than the way his father, Karl, had spelled it.

On the German wedding certificate documenting his true-life marriage to Doris Tanzler, his name reads, "Georg Karl Tanzler." On his certificate of United States citizenship, which he didn't receive until 1950, two years before his death, he legally attempted to change his name to "Carl Tanzler von Cosel." The name change was typed inauspiciously on the back of the certificate.

Von Cosel's memories of his birthplace and early life are clothed in romantic garb:

> I was born [January 12, 1877] in Dresden , Germany, in the town house of our family called the "Castle," but there was another castle, the Villa Cosel, out in the country and it was there I grew up. This later manor had the reputation of being a haunted house and the White Woman, whom my mother told me had appeared from time to time during the past two centuries, was supposed to be my ancestor, the Countess Cosel, who died in 1765. Hers is quite a romantic

history … [and] the beginning of my relationship to Elena.

As a young boy, however, I had no interest in the family tree and the existence of a ghost in the manor was never mentioned to me, not entertained. True enough, at the age of twelve I had a dream, or rather a vision, of a very beautiful girl in a white dress, reclining on a rococo settee, which I painted on a piece of paper then. My boyish interests were … entirely concentrated on electricity, on chemical experiments; and on flying machines, astronomy; in fact, all phenomena of the universe.

While still at high school, fascinated by the saga of the Flying Valkyries, I built myself a glider plane. I tested this contraption from a hill in the park, but then the giggling of the maids embarrassed me so that I continued flying experiments only after midnight to the alarm of superstitious dogs of the peasantry….

By the time I went to college, I had established in the Green Room of the manor a fairly big laboratory for high-voltage electricity. The garden hall I had converted into a workshop wherein I built one boat and two hot-air balloons made from Japanese silk, which it took my mother and a needlewoman months to sew together. I had no interest outside science, music and paintings; girls did not exist for me, except formally, even as I went to University at Leipzig and I did neither smoke nor drink. Time seemed too precious to me for such pursuits of momentary happiness. Engrossed in science after science I took, at the age of twenty-four, final degrees as master of arts in medicine, in philosophy, mathematics, physics, chemistry, etc., having passed nine different examinations beside the S.M.

If true, Count von Cosel was a young genius. However, exactly who Carl Tanzler really was is unclear because the veracity of his memoirs is simply not to be trusted. Partly truth and partly fiction, they were written by a man whose obsessive love for his Elena (whom he believed to be reincarnated in a young dying woman) had warped his sense of reality.

Did he graduate from the University at Leipzig with nine different degrees as he claimed or did he learn by reading everything technical he could get his hands on? The implausible nature of some of his inventions and his tendency toward exaggeration suggest he might well have been self-taught.

It was during his intense, youthful studies that he had a cosmic visitor—the apparition of his bride to be. According to the memoirs, von Cosel's meeting with his beloved Elena took place approximately ten years before she was officially entitled to a birth certificate:

> I was sitting in my chair in the Green Room; piled on the large table were writing materials from the college, books, and laboratory instruments.... Toward the back, the room was divided by a large curtain which enclosed my photographic darkroom wherein I used to develop the X-ray pictures I made.... To complete the picture; all doors, of which the Green Room had several, were locked, except the door to the adjoining music hall, which was furnished splendidly with a Lipp piano, an organ, chairs, chaise-lounge, settees, Florentine table, life-sized Venus de Milo and an easel on which there stood a picture I once painted of Judith, the beautiful Jewess who slew Holofernes. Besides there were several large oil paintings of Italian masters in gold frames hanging on the walls, also ten-feet high mirrors and armor.
>
> The hour was late, about eleven I would say; I felt tired but my day's work was not yet finished. Suddenly, without looking up from my papers, I noticed a movement near my side. It was a pencil lying on the table; it moved slowly half across the table.... Scientific training had taught me the first law in the observance of phenomena; don't change any of the existing conditions.... I merely paid little attention to it and kept bent on my work. Then it lifted itself off of the table, performing a few somersaults in the air and down to the floor. Now a match box started walking about the table, lifting itself, gyrating in the air. Then there followed my books.... My amazement I cannot even try to describe. Finally, the entire heavy oaken table with the papers in my immediate reach sill on it, lifted itself off the floor and floated upward as if carried by water....
> [Then] there was a noise like the report of a gun from the

direction of my static electricity machine. Walking over, to see what had happened, I found that all four huge central glass disks had been broken right through the middle. The outside glass plates of the glass case still were intact and so were the condensers. The damage made me really angry, the expensive machine was now useless....

I was not frightened or anything like that, I still believed in some kind of a prank or maybe that there was a thief or prowler in the house....

While still searching my bedroom, I heard a renewed noise in the Green Room, and in returning there my eyes met the strangest sight; all of the chairs in the room had a lively time moving and poltering about, agitated by an invisible agency. No harm was done and the sight was even funny. I realized that in the face of the supernatural I was rather a ridiculous figure, standing there. But then the harmless dance of the furniture turned into something more malignant: I heard another crash and as I opened the door I found one of my mercury pumps, which I kept there, smashed, its fifty pounds of mercury running over the floor which the splinters of glass floated. This was another heavy damage running into hundreds of dollars, so my anger was aroused....

In the third night, however, I was mysteriously awakened at around 2 a.m. I hardly believed my eyes. There were, however, standing by my bed two women, one bending over my face, a tall lady with snow-white hair, a striking likeness to the portrait of the Countess Anna which I remembered so well. The second figure kept somewhat behind her, as if trying to hide, and the Countess held the reluctant younger lady by the hand. Bending still lower and staring at me, the Countess Anna addressed me as follows:

"I've been trying to get your attention for quite some time, my boy. But you wouldn't take note. You were too much engrossed in your experiments. That's why I had to use some violence.... Look here, Carl, I have brought you the bride whom some day you will meet."

I tried to answer something but I could not speak. I had plenty of words, but I could not open my jaws. The Countess now stepped a little aside and at the same time she drew her companion nearer to me. For a very brief moment, the veil parted from the shrouded figure's face. Spellbound, I saw, framed in long, dark, black tresses, a young girl's face, so beautiful I can't attempt to describe it. For a fleeting second I saw the girl smile at me; a wonderful smile, but at that moment the Countess Anna detached herself from my arm which she had touched and the apparition quite suddenly disappeared.

Strange as this may seem, I was in no way overexcited. It all seemed very natural, if very wonderful to me. With a feeling of relief and quiet happiness, I just noted the time on my clock—two o'clock—and then fell back into sound sleep.

After this first encounter with the supernatural, the Count said he realized how much more there was to learn and discover, how much more work there was to be done in search of knowledge.

This was then the manner in which most people would call the supernatural, entered my life. I did not know at the time that this experience was to be formative for the whole rest of my life. My personal reaction to the experience was wholly scientific. Deny the apparition I could not. Rational explanation I had none. Determined to find a rational explanation, if I could, I started studying the metaphysical classics, in which, until then, I had not interested myself, and the more psychological and spiritual literature. This, however, I found to be of little help; it became increasingly clear that I had to navigate my own course into this vast, unexplored sea, though Kiesewetter and DuPrel's *Metaphysik* gave me a good foundation which is a necessity and safe guide in this field of ethereal phenomena.

And chart his own course he did—"Ulysses in Search of Elena," he termed it in his memoirs—an odyssey that he claimed led him from continent to continent all over the world. An odyssey that led him to his second apparition in the Campo Santo cemetery in Genoa. This time he saw a marble statue of a beautiful girl who bore a striking resemblance to the apparition he had seen in the Green Room. He learned that the girl immortalized in stone had died at the age of twenty-two and that strangely her name had been— Elena.

As if under a spell I kept repeating that name, "Elena, Elena." And it was then that all of sudden the figure of a live girl in the same white dress seemed to detach itself from the statue and slowly walk past where I stood, looking at me. There was no doubt in my mind that she was indeed the apparition of my youthful days and that she was alive.

According to von Cosel it was destiny that led him from Germany to Australia, the first leg of the Odyssey that eventually brought him to Key West.

After many travels in many a land I finally settled down after a fashion in Sydney, Australia, thirteen years before the outbreak of the first World War.

In Sydney, he claimed he "was employed by the Australian Government as a civil engineer and X-ray expert."

I had become a British citizen. I had a good salary and a pleasant home overlooking Darling Point. In the quiet harbor, right in front of my doorstep, there was anchored the big one-hundred-ten-foot power boat, a former torpedo boat I had rebuilt for myself and which I intended to use for deep sea exploration and for fishing expeditions which often led me far into the South Sea Archipelagoes.

Perhaps this was true; perhaps not.

In 1901, if Count Karl was telling the truth, he began living in Australia. He would have been twenty-four years old and that would have been a busy year for the young man—passing nine different examinations at the University, traveling from continent to continent and finally settling down in Sydney, Australia.

His story of having lived in Australia has some credibility. The Count could speak and write English well enough to be understood easily when he reached Key West. In fact, he was fluent enough in the language to land a job at the Marine Hospital. His accent, while definitely German, had a British tilt that probably came from Australia. How and when he got there is unclear.

One invention he claimed to have made while in Australia was a seaplane with a one-hundred-and-ten-foot wing span and two five-hundred-horsepower diesel engines he asserts he was building in 1910.

There was absolutely no way under the sun that a plane was going to fly with two diesel engines of that size—they would have been aeronautically too heavy.

The Wright Brothers had flown their aircraft for the first time at Kitty Hawk, North Carolina, in 1903. No plane has ever flown successfully with diesel engines.

As for his account of the time elements, there are several reasons to doubt that he lived in Australia prior to World War I. While at the Marine Hospital, the Count gave the impression that the only time he had spent in Australia was the time he was incarcerated. A co-worker who remembered the Count's early days at the hospital had no recollection of von Cosel talking about civilian life, nor did he mention that he had ever become a British citizen. She was under the impression that the Count was somehow taken there as a prisoner of war in 1914.

While he may or may not have actually been in Australia before the war, he was visited there, according to his memoirs by new apparitions of his bride-to-be. He was mysteriously awakened as if raised from the dead by a living hand. Twenty months later, at exactly seven p.m.:

> With my mouth still full of food I continued eating, too amazed to do anything else. At first my eyes deceived me but the apparition stood there all right; after looking a second and third time, there could be no doubt about its reality. It was a woman about my own size, and I noted the rich, black hair unrolling over her shoulders, showing through the veils, so long it reached down to her knees. Even through the veil I could see dark eyes which fixedly stared at me; I also noticed that the light from out in the hall faintly showed through her form. A tremble of supreme joy and anxiety shook my frame. There she was at last, the apparition of Castle Cosel, my promised bride.

> By the automatism of habit, I arose from my chair, addressed the lady with the conventional words, "What can I do for you, my lady? What message may you have for me?" She did not answer but for her beautiful face turned into smiles, the most heavenly I have ever seen. Still frozen to the threshold she stretched out both her hands to me, in friendly gesture like a child. As I walked across the room to meet those arms, I felt my hair raising and cold shivers running down my spine, the closer I approached her, and then felt her arms closing around me and felt my arms embracing her. I cannot possibly describe the upsurge of a divine happiness such as I had never experienced before. There was a melting together in divine bliss. Her wonderful dark tresses, fragrant and caressing, covered us both. There were no longer any chills, only elation and warmth, filling my entire body. It was as if my feet went off the ground and she and I were floating in space.... I would have loved nothing better than to stay in this embrace forever; only at this very culmination of my happiness some substance evaporated. The body of the girl dissolved in my arms.... Fear gripped my heart that perhaps I had lost her again, that perhaps she had sacrificed the very substance of her being, poured it all out into this one embrace.

Then followed one of the strangest weeks in von Cosel's life up to then. The apparition stayed with him for seven days while he went about his routine work and ordinary pursuits. Never demanding yet always there, she stood by his bed as he slept at night before vanishing into thin air.

> I have no words to describe my sorrow over her loss; may it suffice to say that mental depression brought my health to a very low state, so that a fortnight thereafter I found myself in a hospital and remained there for more than three months, unconscious most of the time, under a combined attack of typhoid and malaria fever....

This is how von Cosel described the end of the good life "down under."

> I had lived [in Australia] for 15 years.... I was respected

and had good friends everywhere, and yet, as soon as the war broke out, they looked upon me as enemy.

The military moved him, and he lived at military headquarters for five years. When he returned to his home...

The inside was a shambles. The pipe organ was chopped to pieces with an ax. I lost my library, all of my documents, my collections of diamonds, emeralds, and opals. I had some big ones, fiery opals as big as that.

However, another version of the truth may be that von Cosel was in the German army. Von Cosel reportedly told Dr. Alvan Foraker that he had been an officer in the German submarine division. According to several people, including Tom Hambright, historian at the Monroe County Library, von Cosel received a monthly check that he picked up at the post office. Its mysterious source adds to the questions surrounding his past. It could have been a pension for his military service.

He was twenty-three at the turn of the century, thirty-five at the beginning of the First World War when he claimed he was taken into custody and interned in Australia at the Trial Bay Concentration Camp. In 1939 Carl von Cosel published in the *Rosicrucian Digest* an article titled "The Trial Bay Organ—a Product of Wit and Ingenuity." The editor's note preceding the article states:

"Many years ago, Carl von Cosel travelled from India to Australia with the intention of proceeding to the South Sea Islands. He paused in Australia to collect equipment and suitable boats, and to become acquainted with prevailing weather and sea conditions. However, he became interested in engineering and electrical work there, bought property, boats, an organ, an island in the Pacific—so that he was still in Australia at the end of ten years. He had just begun to build a trans-ocean flyer when the war broke out and the British military authorities placed him in a concentration camp for 'safekeeping,' along with many officers from India and China who were prisoners of war. Later he was removed to Trial Bay."

In the article, which follows the publication's question of the day, "Should Women Whose Husbands are Employed be Banned from the Business World?" von Cosel writes:

It was a bright morning that followed a stormy night in March, 1917, when I was strolling down the Rocks toward the beach of Trial Bay. The storm that had screamed and roared though the turrets of our castle all night long reminded me of a peculiar similar stormy night at my home in Darling Point, Sydney, which terminated in the appearance of a beautiful white veiled spirit (Aeyesha). This time, however, nothing of that kind happened, and besides it would not be a suitable place for a beautiful woman to appear as we were a lot of men packed together from all parts of the world and interned as prisoners of war.

Each morning the bugle called us for the roll call in the prison yard. After this we went to the dining hall for breakfast, and the great iron gates were opened so that we could go down to the seashore until five o'clock in the afternoon. At that hour there was another roll call and the gates were closed for the night to prevent anyone from "harming" or "stealing" us, so they said.

Now the gates were open and I was going down to the water. The storm had calmed down but there were still smooth rolling seas from the Pacific running in among the heavy boulders of granite-stone along the picturesque shoreline of the peninsula on which our prison, with its five white turrets and high stone walls, was built.

Searching among the boulders, I discovered long planks from ships, wedged deep in between the stones by the force of the dashing breakers. After some difficulty I managed to extricate these and haul them away to a place higher up, just above the line of highest water, where I commenced to build a castle on the rocks.

This so-called "castle" consisted merely of a leveled off terrace of granite stones with back against the rocks, closed up on each end by a wall about three feet thick, with door openings. The roof joined the back surface of the rocks and rested on the walls on either side, while the front of the terrace was open so as to overlook the entire horizon of the Pacific Ocean. Along the sea side I raised up a wall three feet in height and about three feet thick, to guard against falling and to stop the incoming spray. On top of this breast-wall I rested columns to support the roof.

On the other side of the castle, near the beach, I found a large black looking piece of log, about four feet thick, and round, and about the same length. It must have been tossed and rolled about for years by the seas and all edges had been rounded off very smoothly, like a ball, through the continuous grinding of the sand and the pumice stone, which is floating on the water in great quantities. This piece of a tree stump proved to be a very fine red cedar.

It came into my mind at once that I might use it to carve out an organ and I could almost see the instrument ready before me. All that was needed was to work out the measurements and details and to obtain the additional materials required for such work. For the present, there were no tools to do anything with, except the woodchopper axes from the kitchen and cross cut saws. All tools in our possession had been confiscated long ago. Still I had my pocket knife left, at least, and my shaving kit with razor, and an odd file. We did not use razors very much as our toilet was indeed a very primitive one. We gave the appearance of having returned to the stone-age type of humanity. If it had not been for our own splendid institutions, high college, small university theater, and our good orchestra, our conception and memory of civilization would have been severely shaken. Even the sight of a woman or a child had become to us something like a dream of long ago. Blessed the one among us who still had a picture of such a treasured being. He was eagerly watched for, just to get a look at that picture!

I am only trying to give a fairly true view of the conditions we were living under, and the state of our minds as a result of such isolation for a length of time. Each of us had the inclination to do something, but what? It proved a great difficulty for many to get over that profound weariness and they helplessly brooded away to a lethargy bordering on insanity, the tropical sun and heat of Australia helping toward such drowsiness.

The lengthy article goes on to detail the organ's construction and the difficulty he had in building it with his meager tools. Later, when the armistice was signed and he was forced to repatrate to Germany, von Cosel claimed the instrument accompanied him on the voyage and that the ship encountered weather so foul he constantly "feared for the organ, my most valued possession."

The thought of all the endless labor being lost troubled me, but thinking of all that I had to leave behind in Sydney— all my boats, my beautiful instruments, organs, etc., which perhaps I never would see again—consoled me a little. I was of one mind again with my Indian friends that all earthly goods are made to come and go and are continuously in a process of change and transformation, the spirit being the only lasting power.

When rounding Cape Lewin everyone on board became seasick and a grippe-patient, and our ship was turned into a floating hospital. On the way across the Indian Ocean, we lost one life every day and twenty-four men were buried at sea. The worst of it was that every dead body had to be carried through our dining room rather than being cast overboard on the aft deck close to the hospital, as this was the women's and children's quarter.

All that time we had very bad seas, lasting the whole distance to Durban, South Africa, and the ship had been badly knocked about. I thought that when the ship sank I would look for my organ case, as the great many air-boxes would maintain a very good floating capacity. It certainly would make an ideal life raft on account of its flat shape and its many hollow organ pipes, which would take a long time to fill with water as each on singly had been securely wrapped in paper, and besides, Australian cedar wood possesses a very great floating capacity.

However, the weather cleared up at Durban and we had a fine trip the remaining four weeks while rounding the Cape of Africa and going north through the Atlantic to Plymouth,

Dover, and Rotterdam in Holland.

In due course we arrived at Dover from where we Germans were then trans-shipped to Rotterdam. Two years after the armistice. I arrived with my organ at the old manor house in Saxony. During the fifteen years of my travels, father had died and one of my two sisters had married in America. Only mother, now very old, and my youngest sister welcomed me home.

When I was still in the concentration camp I had fancied, like most of the others that it would be possible to pick up the threads of the old life after the war. Reality, of course, was different. I was working on some inventions, worked out while in prison camp, but found they could not be used owing to war restrictions. Most of my old professors from my student days had died; the intellectual life at the universities which I had cherished so much I found to be in a state of depression. The whole country bore the stamp of defeat. I felt as if I were a burden to the meager resources of the family estate which were barely sufficient for mother and sister. With my newly acquired patents of inventions, and *Reichs Entechadigung*, I decided to accept my mother's wish to go to America to my sister.

According to von Cosel, the organ at this point was placed once again in its case and transshipped to the United States.

Assuming von Cosel arrived in Germany two years after the armistice as he claimed, there are six years, from 1920 until the year he immigrated, 1926, that are totally unaccounted for in his writings. His retrospective account of his past neglected to mention his marriage to Doris, the birth of their daughters, or their subsequent immigration.

Mrs. Tanzler, in her passport picture, was a handsome lady and the two children were adorable. They looked like a happy family, full of expectations on their way to meet their father, Carl Tanzler, to begin a new and exciting life in a prosperous new land.

Von Cosel claimed he was of noble birth, but whether he was in reality a member of German nobility is another intriguing aspect of his life. One of the people who knew him and worked with him while he was here insisted that the Count must have been a nobleman because she personally saw his title inscribed on a pocket watch of which von Cosel was very proud. His co-worker described it as a large timepiece with four diamonds in the center of the gold cover that protected the face. Inscribed on the inside was, "Count von Cosel from the Czar of Russia." The fellow worker's memory of the watch was still vivid because the Count, in a moment of grandiose generosity and with great flair tried to give it to Dr. Lombard as a gift. When the doctor wouldn't accept such an expensive present, the Count gave it to Dr. Lombard's wife, Marion, who accepted it reluctantly when there was no way to refuse gracefully.

One rebuttal to his claim of nobility, however, came from a surviving family member who said, "it was just something he made up."

Perhaps Carl Tanzler somehow came into possession of the watch while in Germany and kept it. Then later, when he decided to become a Count in America, where no one would know the difference, he began to show it about. His memoirs make no mention of his friendship with the Czar of Russia who was murdered during the Russian Revolution of 1917. More than a few Europeans have upgraded their lineage while in the United States to impress the impressionable. It is quite possible that, like them, Carl Tanzler desperately wanted to be somebody he wasn't.

Reinforcing the reality of his commoner status are records that show Karl Tanzler was born in a modest home in Dresden, Germany. Supporting the theory of switched identities, there actually exists a von Cosel castle in Dresden, Germany, and there was a von Cosel clan with a distinctive coat of arms.

Somehow both birthplaces survived the firebombing by the allies near the end of World War II although the castle was badly damaged by the air attacks.

Noble or not, as a child Karl undoubtedly liked science and read scientific literature. Whether he was a genius or merely a good talker is debatable. Either way or in between, he was able to understand scientific language and use it in a credible manner.

Chapter Four

Diagnosis and Prognosis

COUNT von Cosel considered himself a medical doctor and told the Marine Hospital administration that he was one. Even though the hospital found this not to be true, they allowed him to move up from the position of attendant to technician. Under the severe scrutiny of Dr. Lombard and the other physicians on his staff, the Count proved he was more than capable of operating the X-ray equipment and doing laboratory work as well as taking blood samples. It seemed not to have mattered that he was a German citizen working in a United States government facility.

"Thunderstruck," he was walking on air after his and Elena's initial meeting when he pierced her delicate finger. He was jubilant when he learned that Elena, the same woman/child who had appeared, he was certain, so often to him as an apparition, would be coming in the next day for a chest X-ray.

Early that next morning, he made sure his tie was on straight and the clothes he wore were pressed to perfection. On his way to the hospital, the whole world around him seemed alive with excitement. The sun's early heavenly rays danced off of the lush tropical foliage—the scheffleras, the poinciana trees and the mahogany trees glistened in the morning light.

At the hospital, he prepared his equipment more thoroughly than ever. Concentration was difficult as he dealt with the other patients scheduled before the Cuban beauty with raven black hair arrived.

After what seemed an eternity, Elena was escorted in. The Count stood with military bearing as she entered the room.

"Good morning Miss Hoyos," he said with a professional air and bowed slightly. She seated herself on the varnished oak chair next to the table where her records were being examined by this interesting looking, cultured gentleman with the European accent.

Though he had looked over her charts so many times he knew what they said by heart; he pretended to scrutinize them thoroughly and glanced as often as he dared at the patient noting her chest moving out and then back again with each labored breath.

"You have been coughing, is this so, Miss Hoyos?"

"Yes, doctor, but I slept better last night than I have for a while. I barely coughed at all this morning."

"I think this is good," he said looking at her brown eyes, which were staring down at the pine wood floor in front of her.

"My doctor said that you will be able to tell me if I have tuberculosis."

"Yes, yes indeed, medicine is very advanced these days. My laboratory is equipped with the most modern equipment," the doctor said with an aristocratic-sounding German accent that made the "th's" sound like soft "z's." "Zis procedure will not take long, I assure you. It is absolutely painless. Your hand, Miss Hoyos," he said calmly even though his heart was beginning to flutter. The soft touch of her almond colored skin made him perspire slightly as he positioned his fingers on her wrist in order to take her pulse. With his right hand, he pulled out a plain gold pocket watch from his vest. At this moment, he wished he hadn't given his large, diamond studded one to Dr. Lombard's wife. He wished he could give it to his Elena.

"Your pulse is normal, a little fast, but that is to be expected. This often happens when the patient sees the doctor's white coat," he said with a trace of a smile on his face trying to make conversation. Rising from his chair positioned close to Elena, Count von Cosel took the stethoscope that was hanging around his neck and placed the ends in his ears. Then, he placed the cold metal disk on her back between her shoulder blades. Savoring each heartbeat, he moved the disk approximately every ten seconds.

"Unbutton the top button of your blouse, Miss Hoyos," he said firmly before placing his stethoscope on the smooth skin below her collar bone on the right side and then the left side of her body, slightly above her chest at the top of her lungs. Because of her anxiety she was inhaling and exhaling more rapidly than before. "Dr." von Cosel was having some difficulty breathing himself.

"Can you tell me anything?" Elena asked anxiously. It was uncomfortable for her to have a strange man's hand touching her skin.

"Yes, of course, I am the doctor, am I not? I hear the lungs having a little bit hard time breathing. Not so bad. It's good you are feeling better. The X-rays will tell us everything. Let me says this, I have studied pulmonary tuberculosis very thoroughly and will be able to see any lesions that may appear on the film. Tuberculosis is a strange disease. If you have it, and we don't know this yet, but if you do, I can treat it. Don't be afraid."

Positioning himself behind the apparatus, he ordered her to sit in front of the weird looking device.

"Come, sit here....

"Sit straight. It is important that you stay as still as you possibly can while I take the X-rays. When I tell you, take a deep breath and hold it. Your enemy is a dangerous and invisible one. The more I know, the better I will be able to treat it. When I turn off the light, you must take off your blouse and your undergarments."

After a pause, "Doctor, are you certain this is necessary?"

"The X-ray machine will photograph your lungs. For the X-rays to see properly, nothing can come between me and my machine, and I'm the only one who can work it. There will be only faint illumination as the X-ray machine takes the photographs. I will not turn the lights back on until you have put on your blouse."

Even though the room was darkened, there was a dim red light that was part of the equipment. Elena's eyes looked down at the buttons as she quietly undid them, one by one. By dropping her shoulder, the soft cotton garment slipped down so she could pull her arms from the sleeves.

Carl Tanzler, under the cover of the dark room, wiped his brow with his handkerchief. His heart was pounding with love so abounding, the only way he was able to maintain his composure was by fidgeting with the radioactive camera. Though his head was positioned as if he were looking elsewhere, his eyes were looking at Elena as she removed the straps of her slip from her shoulders and pulled the silken fabric down around her waist exposing the young, perfectly-shaped breasts that her husband had, in the beginning, found so erotic—before she started coughing.

Looking down at her own body, Elena became lost in her thoughts for a moment. Her mind couldn't escape the pleasures she had enjoyed with the man waiting for her in the other room. How sad the love between them had gone cold when she started coughing. It seemed like ages ago that they, holding on to each other, rocking back and forth, had conceived a child. She hardly noticed the doctor as he instructed her to put her hands on her hips and sit straight. It was as though she were someone else sitting there naked from the waist up in front of this strange man and his strange camera.

"That wasn't so bad, was it?" asked von Cosel a little too cheerfully as he turned on the bright lights.

He added, "Miss Hoyos, rest assured I am going to do everything in my power to keep you in good health. You have my word. Eat well. Get plenty of rest. Follow my instructions explicitly and everything will be fine. I know this has been a difficult time for you. I will let you know the results as soon as I develop the film. I am interested in your case because I believe my machines and I have the power to cure your illness and make medical history. You must rest," he implored emphatically. "And I must analyze the results carefully in order to draw the correct scientific conclusion. The diagnosis and prognosis is most important. I will see you tomorrow." He gave a half bow.

When she had gone von Cosel's eyes focused on the developing tray and the film as he transferred it from one tray to another. His nostrils smelled the chemicals and the antiseptic odors of the room, but his mind wasn't paying much attention to the information. His mind saw only the bare image of the woman he had fallen hopelessly, forever and ever, head-over-heels in love with. His senses smelled only her perfume.

Then, abruptly, the romantic vision gave way to sadness when he saw lesions confirming tuberculosis. The realization that Elena might not have long to live shot through his heart like an arrow.

I saw her the very next day, when she came in for more tests and this time I took a radiograph of her lungs which brought me the painful revelation that she was suffering from tuberculosis. From the frailty of her figure, from the listlessness with which she sat, I had suspected that much from the very first day. The certainty which now was gained increased my worries because our hospital was not adequately equipped for the treatment of lung tuberculosis, yet some way had to be found to help her; a fierce determination to aid her, to bring her back to health was burning in my soul. Both Elena and her mother could not fail to observe my deepest interest in her case. They invited me to the family home, and needless to say, I went there that very evening. It was a very small dilapidated home to which I came; the family was poor. Elena's father worked in a tobacco factory. There were two sisters, both very different from Elena. Her mother, a good-hearted, if simple woman, and numbers of young people of all ages, whose relationship to the family I could never ascertain.

Elena sitting very quietly, and obviously feeling far from well, in a chair in the kitchen, shone like the sun amongst all these lesser human stars....

Days later I went again to her house, in order to take a blood test. This time I was led by her mother into her room. There, to my utter surprise and joy, I discovered hanging over her bed a picture of Saint Cecilia playing the organ, the same Saint Cecilia to whom I had brought roses in the Catacombs of Rome. Still treating me as if I were a teacher, which I indeed was, and she my little pupil, Elena said:

"That's Saint Cecilia, sir."

"Yes, and you know, Elena, she is my guardian angel, and this is the first time that I've seen her picture here in America."

"We too," said Elena, "are not Americans. We came from Cuba several years ago."

As in a blinding revelation I now had the explanation for the spell under which I had watched the Carnival in Havana four years ago and I also had won the certainty that it was my guardian angel, Saint Cecilia, who had brought me and Elena together.

All this inner happiness, notwithstanding my worries as a doctor mounted steadily. Since our hospital lacked the equipment I wished to use for Elena and moreover I considered the Florida climate as unfavorable for her condition, I proposed to send her at my own expense, of course, to some famous tuberculosis institution abroad where I was reasonably certain she would be cured. This offer she refused because, in the first place, with the euphoria so typical with tuberculosis patients, she did not realize the seriousness of her condition. This left me only one choice; I had to procure at least the electrical equipment to treat her right on the spot. I wrote to several firms for the necessary apparatus and some of it I started building myself. In the meantime, I decided to give her radiation therapy with the hospital equipment, although the service outfit was not powerful enough for deep radiation therapy. Whatever was left of my spare time I spent on the completion of an airplane I had started to construct some time ago.

There is little doubt that Carl Tanzler von Cosel exuded brilliance to those around him. His theories and analytical medical skills impressed the doctors and nurses at the hospital. Perhaps as some later observed, he was walking the tightrope between genius and mad scientist without a net. The Count, even though he may have had a valid foundation for his theories, wasn't able to translate these theories into working inventions.

The airplane he had begun constructing behind the Marine Hospital was a prime example. There were two conflicting stories about the partially finished airship that vaguely resembled the *Spirit of St. Louis,* the first aircraft to successfully fly across the Atlantic Ocean. Von Cosel claimed he had built this ship from scratch. The more likely explanation, however, was that he bought a wrecked airplane, hauled it behind the hospital, and was trying to restore it. At th time there was a surprisingly large amount of aeronautical activity in Key West. Aeromarine Airways, Inc., using seaplanes, provided passenger and mail service to and from Cuba in the early 1920's. Pan American Airways made its first commercial flight from Key West to Havana in 1927.

Those who remember his small plane always comment on the big wheels. In the photographs, they appear to be about the same height as von Cosel himself, approximately five-foot-seven or —eight inches tall. They look to be about a foot-and-a-half thick and were hollow. Von Cosel claimed they were superior to pontoons and that they would allow him, upon completion of the airplane, to operate it on land and on water.

Von Cosel talked convincingly about ratios, relativity, gravity, and the density of air versus water displacement. Still, his inventions invariably came up short.

Regular, stationary pontoons, in addition to being aerodynamically superior, don't rotate the way a wheel does. Von Cosel's pontoon/wheels did not take the rear section of the aircraft into consideration. Without a third wheel the same size on the rear of the airplane, the tail would sink and the nose would point up toward the sky as it rolled the rest of the way over, leaving only the wheels above water. There was simply no way a plane could float or fly the way he had designed the wheels that he attached to the landing gear struts.

Once Elena had regained her health, this plane was to take the two of us to a South Sea island which I had discovered for myself during one of my fishing expeditions in Australia. This was a little paradise and my dream was that Elena and I should spend our honeymoon there. Every time she came to the hospital for treatment, we took time out to inspect the plane together. Those moments were of great delight for both of us, when we sat side by side in the little pilot's cabin and imagined how it would be when it carried us into the air and across the ocean.

"What name are you going to give the ship?" she asked.

"I wish you would permit me to name our ship La Contesa de Cosel."

Elena blushed, for this was the first time I had intimated my wish to marry her.

"All right," she said, "let's name her *Contesa Elena.*"

One morning, von Cosel carefully painted:

Cts Elaine von Cosel C-3

on the crackled silver paint between the starboard side window and the engine cowling. The plane had only one small window for the pilot to see forward through.

Poor Elena. Not only was he going to build machines to cure her, one day, he promised, she would fly in his airplane to some island in the middle of the Pacific Ocean eight thousand miles away.

Eventually, in a strange way, that prophecy would come partially true.

Chapter Five

Treatments, Proposals and Roses

Despite her condition, Elena's beauty had not faded. If anything it had been enhanced by the tragedy of her illness, which rested in the darkness of her eyes.

Her parents were beside themselves with worry. What could be worse than learning your precious daughter has contracted a terminal illness? They were angry at her husband, Luis, for leaving her; however, because she was in poor health, the anger and frustration they felt toward him paled in comparison to the horrible news their beautiful child was desperately sick with tuberculosis. At night, sleep for them stayed so near the surface that it wasn't much different from being awake, and they cried often as the days got longer and the summer heat settled in. The strain was taking its toll on Elena's mother and father and all of those around them. The financial repercussions of their poor luck were even more depressing.

There was barely enough money to get by in normal times. Costly medical treatment meant tremendous hardship. How much could they spare? What would it cost? How could they not do everything in their power to save her?

And then along came the Count, the medicine man with all the answers. Was he a knight in shining armor brandishing a sword or Don Quixote charging windmills? They didn't know. Perhaps their prayers had been answered now that their daughter's health had become his mission.

Elena's parents were in a most vulnerable mental state, and von Cosel not only seemed knowledgeable about her illness and how to treat it, he wasn't charging them for his services.

Next in importance to the X-ray treatment was to build

up her physical strength. Every day now I brought her fruit and some of the finest medicinal wine I could procure; I even went to the priest, because he was able to get the kind of wine for me which I wanted for my sick Elena.

With these combined means the tubercular infiltration for the time was checked, even with the minor equipment of the hospital, and Elena's general condition was improving.

Until this time, Carl Tanzler had been sending his real family in Zephyrhills part of his paycheck. Before Elena, there was money to spare, but now that she was in the picture, the checks became sporadic until they ended altogether. A co-worker at the hospital who thought she knew him well remembered the Count talking about letters he received from a relative asking for money. He discussed the request with her but was vague about who the relative making the request was. At the hospital he said nothing about Doris or the girls growing up without a father.

Dr. Lombard knew there was little hope of recovery, but he apparently didn't discourage von Cosel's genuine efforts to find the miracle cure. After a while as Elena continued to weaken, her parents became skeptical and, at times, resented the arrogant, condescending way von Cosel treated them, but what else could they do? Without him, there was no one, nothing. Meanwhile Elena, who had been pampered even when she was in good health, refused to accept the seriousness of her condition.

In fact, she told me she didn't really believe she was sick at all. I cautioned her as best I could, but unfortunately her family, too, arrived at the wrong conclusion that their daughter was now cured and that my continuation of the treatment was more or less a pretext to be as much as possible with Elena.

Von Cosel pressed his case, both medically and personally.

Her twenty-first birthday approached; I had high hopes now that she would accept me as her suitor, as she had allowed me to buy the ring. I brought it over that day, hidden in a bouquet of roses. I also brought cakes and wine and we had a wonderful day together....

As they talked and laughed on that isolated happy day, von Cosel told her of his deep feelings for her.

> "Elena, I can give you so much more than someone your age. I can give you my science, my experience, my capacity to save your life—all of this and more—I will give you my Undying Love."

But Elena countered: "Carlos, I am a married woman. Yes, he left me, and true, I will probably never see him again, but that doesn't mean that I'm not married in the eyes of God and the church."

Von Cosel tried to entice her: "Don't you want to get well? Don't you want to see the world? I will fly you in our airship to my South Sea island where the lush green mountains rise from the indigo ocean."

She gave a little laugh and joked, "You're going to fly me in your plane with no wings?"

She had offended the doctor. "I can build wings. I am building a high-power, high-frequency unit with ray equipment; surely I can build wings so we can fly away together. I can fly you above the atmosphere where the ultra-violet rays from space will surely cure you." It was then he learned that Elena might not be ignorant of her real condition.

Elena's beautiful face took on a look of pain. "Carl, I think I'm dying."

"No don't believe that. You're not going to heaven yet. But don't worry, if you die, I'll take you in my arms. The good Lord will take us both to heaven."

"Bring me my fan, please, Carlos. I used it when we danced, when I was still able, when I danced at my wedding. Carl ... I'm frightened."

"Elena, forget about him. You were meant to be with me. It's our destiny. Of course, there is no way you could know, but you've been looking for me longer than you've been alive. I'm sure of it. I'm positive. You appeared to me when I was only twelve years old. I was playing the organ at our castle in Germany when a violent thunderstorm blew across the countryside. Before the storm I was playing pianissimo. Then, as the thunder crashed, I began playing full organ fortissimo. The wind blew the door open. It was you, Elena, who rushed through the door, kissed me, and ... vanished."

Elena gave him a sad look.

"Carl, I don't know what you're talking about. How could I look for you before I was born? Let me get well first. Then we'll see what happens."

In an effort to be nice to the doctor, he was invited to Elena's sister's wedding (another expenditure the Hoyos family could ill afford).

When I got there late in the afternoon, the marriage ceremony was long since over, but an enormous party was in full swing. The little house was over-crowded with guests, all eating and drinking, and as the hostess for all these people acted my Elena. She hardly took time out to take me by the hand to introduce me to the groom and guests, before she carried on carrying the trays around, serving the drinks, operating the gramophone, and doing a thousand other tasks. It was agonizing for me to sit there by the side of the bride, trying to entertain her as best I could, while, through the clouds of smoke, through the laughter and the gramophone songs, I heard the dry cough of my Elena, who should rest her lungs above all.

The evening seemed like an eternity. It was near midnight when the guests departed and my exhausted girl sat down for a moment by my side.

"Elena," I said, "I admire you, you are the most wonderful hostess in the world. But this sort of thing just can't go on. Permit me to help you. Let's get married and let's get away from all this."

Before she could answer, her mother, whom I had not seen all evening, stood in front of us:

"No daughter of mine is going to marry an American. It is to be a Cuban, if she ever marries again."

With her head bowed, my Elena sat in silence. I took her hand and all I could say was:

"God bless you, and good night, my Elena."

Von Cosel left but he did not give up.

The next time I went over, I brought her a pearl necklace. I had sent my big radio console to her house, hoping that good music would cheer her up. Whenever I found her in a depressed mood, which was often, I took out of my pockets some new present for her; one day a large pendant of rock crystal, the next a pair of earrings, and again a beautiful carved rose of pink coral on a gold chain. Almost every day I wrote her letters, wherein medical advice was strangely mixed with my love for her.

> *My darling Elena,*
> *Please don't deceive yourself that all is well, even if you feel that way, don't throw caution into the wind; your enemy is an invisibly one, he can only be seen by trained, scientific eyes, and he can only be fought in a scientific manner. I know, there are quacks around who are suggesting all kind of magic cures which have their common source in ignorance. Please, take the medicine I am sending and do come back to the hospital for a new check up. Dr. Lombard, too, wants to see you. I am working on our airplane in my spare time. It is now nearly completed and the next time you come, I will give you a key for the cabin and we shall officially christen it. And then too, I am already collecting all the things we are going to need on our wedding trip. Silk dresses for you and a bridal gown which is all white silk, and all the rest of your trousseau, even lingerie and silver slippers and last but not least all of your medicines, like chinosol and adrenaline, glucose, beef extract, and all the rest of it.*
> *Forever yours,*
> *Carl*

"Chinosol" is a bright-yellow, antiseptic, disinfectant and bactericide that, according to a study done by Lederly Laboratories published in 1674 had been used internally with some success in pulmonary tuberculosis. The study went on to say that anyone who doubted the beneficial properties of chinosol, "is either an ignoramus or has interested motives." German doctors continued using it to treat the illness in the early 1900's.

"Adrenaline" is still being used to relieve asthma, bronchitis, emphysema and other pulmonary diseases, so it appears that at least some of Carl's prescriptions were in line with other contemporary medical doctors.

Von Cosel treated Elena at the Marine Hospital where he worked until she began missing appointments and making excuses about why she couldn't come. Elena's family had begun to distrust von Cosel and they started taking her to other doctors and avoiding the Count's efforts to treat her.

> One day her excuse was that her father temporarily had no car. I sent a taxi over, still she refused, saying that she didn't trust the taxi company. My own car had just been stolen, so I borrowed another, but even when I came myself to fetch her, Elena would not come to the hospital. It dawned on me that some kind of an opposition had developed against me and the hospital people within her family.

Von Cosel's claim that his car had been stolen was interesting because a stolen car in 1930 in Key West would have been the theft of the decade and quite an accomplishment without roads leading off of the island. He supposedly owned an old Buick with the back converted into a truck bed. Nothing appeared in the *Key West Citizen* concerning this theft, and it would have been in the crime report and perhaps the headlines had it really happened.

However, Elena's mother had been quite serious when she told von Cosel she wanted Elena to marry another Cuban.

> That this [opposition] was only too true was proved a little later, when again I found the house crowded with young Cubans, even married with happy families, noisy with radio music and full of cigar smoke. I could not help to observe how Elena suffered and it made me mad. I told them they should at least refrain from smoking. This hurt the Spanish pride of her father. The old man made quite a scene about my interfering with his guests:
> "My daughter is quite well and if you don't like smoking, why don't you get out of the house."

That settled things for some time at least. Elena's eyes followed me as I left the house as if to say:

"Suffer it for me."

Not to see her was torture and to be unable to do anything for her was worse. Night after night I dreamed of her, until after a week I got a little note from her:

Dear Doctor:

I am very sorry, because I know how unpleasant your last visit to our home must have been. Please, do forgive us. I'm sure father did not really mean what he said to you. He had been on edge all day and had been very cross with everyone. Please, understand that he didn't mean to be that rude. Both my family and myself would be only too glad to have you as our guest again.

So, please, accept my apology for the other night, you must see us soon.

Your friend,
Elena Hoyos

After that, of course, I could not stay away. What did I care after all about what people said or did. Her life was so much more important than a physician's pride.

Nobody was there except Elena and her mother. I found my Elena in an appalling condition. She lay in a state of serious convulsions on her bed, trembling and gasping for air. Her mother kept her covered with blankets. Determined to find out what had happened, I insisted on an explanation. The frightened mother finally came out with the truth: Elena had just been brought home from another doctor, who had been giving her injections for the past few weeks.

"What kind of injections?" I asked. "And who is the doctor?" She gave me an empty vial and named the doctor. This is a thing, of course, which many patients do: to go behind the back of one physician to another. This man was not a quack, but since he was not informed of my treatment and had started on a different one, the two of us worked at cross purposes and the harm to the patient was being done.

Despite von Cosel's persistence, Elena's mother continued her campaign to lure her captive daughter away from his attentions.

> Scores of cousins thronged the little house at all hours of the day and night; incessantly the radio blared and some sort of a celebration seemed always to be going on. Instead of enjoying the quiet of a hospital which should have been hers, my Elena was damned to live as if in a railroad station.
>
> For a long time now I had realized that there was only one way to have this radically changed, and that was for me to marry her. Time and again, I told her so but she always gave me the same answer:
>
> "But we can't marry, dear, I am not divorced yet, and even if I were divorced, you can't marry a sickly girl, such as me. First let me get well again."

In von Cosel's daydreams, Elena lived quietly with him as he could give her the constant care she so desperately needed. He imagined treating her with single-minded devotion and tender caresses. He blamed her parents when, once again, she began missing appointments for her treatment.

> With much persuasion, I managed to get her once more to the hospital. There I took another series of X-ray pictures which made it absolutely clear that her lungs had worsened. I also took a slow bucky-diaphragm picture of the trunk, including the larynx and thorax cavities. To make the best of it, I simultaneously gave her general radiation. Dr. Lombard, who knew of my great interest in Elena, came over and enjoined me in entreating her to come for treatment regularly— to no avail.

If the bride of his dreams wouldn't come to the hospital, von Cosel knew it was time to take his powerful transformer to her home. It was imperative that she receive intense electrical therapy as soon as possible. Unfortunately, when the Count asked the family if he might install the apparatus, they objected vehemently, calling the odd-looking machine the work of the devil. He couldn't seem to convince them that her life was at stake.

At night, during the few hours he did sleep, von Cosel now had nightmares about Elena's worsening condition.

All I could do, while I was helpless, was to dream of Elena and these dreams became more and more frightening. Once I saw her, very pale and dressed in rags, walking alone behind a high iron fence as if of a penitentiary. I found myself on the other side and cried to her: "Oh, darling, I am so happy I found you at last. Run, darling, run quick, farther down the iron rails I can see a little opening between the bars, it's just big enough for you to crawl through." She held her arms out as if to embrace me, I could drink one kiss from her lips. Then she started running and came following me along; it seemed like an eternity until we arrived at a place where one of those bars was missing—and there she came out into my arms, kissing me.

When I wrote her about this dream, she instructed her sister to go to the hospital and tell me to dream no more.

But how could anyone including the Count stop his dreams?

I had wandered into the countryside outside Key West and had come to a deep gulch with lots of underbrush on the embankment and water at the bottom. There I saw what looked like a bundle of clothing and discovered that it was a human body with the head buried in the mud. The dress looked familiar and as I quickly slid down the embankment, it really was Elena. I turned her over and her face was covered with blood and mud. I washed it with my handkerchief, always rinsing it in the water. At least her features became clear and I could see that only the bridge of her nose had been broken, but that there still was life in her. I took her into my arms and laid her on the higher ground. There I did everything to bring her back to life and at the same time to clean her dress. I needed water, so I stepped down again into the gulch and saw all of a sudden, that there were more bodies lying in the muddy stream, men, women, and children, but they were all dead and in a bad state of decay. I counted thirty-seven bodies in all. They made my hair stand on end because I thought they must all have been murdered and dumped and hidden here. So I fled and took the unconscious body of Elena in my arms to my laboratory. I had just placed her on the X-ray table to examine her for internal injuries when I woke up. SO BEGAN the year 1931....

Again, he wrote to Elena ... begging:

> Darling, if you have any willpower left, please, use it in the right direction, concentrate everything on your health. Please, do come over for treatment before it is too late.
> Let me see you again, Elena, I implore you. So often you have said that I am too old for you, but listen, darling, I never count my years, neither do I count yours. If you were a mummy, five thousand years old, I would marry you just the same. I swear; it's not for selfish reasons that I want this marriage but because I can do so much more than a boy your age.... Oh, darling, I would take you to my South Sea Island or to the big cities of Europe or wherever you want to go. Only do come and let me care for you again.

Elena's condition was becoming critical. Allowing von Cosel to return and treat her were acts of desperation on Mr. and Mrs. Hoyos's part only because von Cosel still offered hope for a cure.

The other medical doctors who were asked to treat Elena were understandably pessimistic about her chances of recovery. The only medication they could offer were pain killers that would make Elena as comfortable as possible as the disease brought her closer to death. This going behind his back, seeing other doctors made von Cosel insanely jealous, especially so in light of the fact that he wasn't a medically recognized "doctor." It was only natural for him to strongly discourage it.

After another of his periodic expulsions, the Count claimed that his beloved and her family had moved from their home on Watson and United Streets to a new home. Unable to find where they lived, von Cosel was inconsolable.

> I buried myself in work as best I could, automaton-like. Night after night I wandered through the town, peering

secretly through the curtains of those innumerable little homes of the poorer sections, always hoping to find her and in vain. Her silence was wearing me down.

Once again, according to von Cosel, fate intervened!

One night, an elderly Spanish lady beckoned to me from the porch of her house and coming near, I recognized in her a woman I had seen with Elena's family.

"Your girl is very, very sick," she told me in a whisper. "The family has moved there-and-there. Elena is now in bed all the time, she needs you, but her parents won't let you come. I tell you what, doctor: it's a crime. Don't you pay any attention to the old folks. You just walk in and if you are still able to, help her. Wait, I'll just lock my door and then I'll show you the house where she lives.

Thank God he had found her again because it was obvious that she needed him now more than ever.

Chapter Six

Where There's Life, There's Hope

Elena was pale and emaciated, wearing the silk kimono he had given her as a present. When Mrs. Hoyos lashed out at him for coming there, the Count, like the hero of a melodrama about to foil the foul villain, lashed back,

> If anybody had tried to stop me, I think, I would have used violence. Right in the hallway I saw her sweet little face, looking straight into my eyes from a chair in the kitchen corner. I cried: "Elena, let me come in."
>
> "Yes, doctor, do come, I'm so glad you are here...."
>
> "Good evening, good evening, mother; I am so happy I found my Elena again. Tell me, what doctor is attending to her now?"
>
> Angrily her mother burst out: "I am her doctor now."
>
> I laughed a little bitterly: "You are some doctor, mother. I am sure you are a good nurse but not a doctor. I have come to stay. From now on you might as well consider me in charge for good."
>
> I left them standing open-mouthed and turned to my bride: "Please, darling, tell me whatever you wish or need at the moment and I will go and bring it to you."

Then, according to his memoirs, she, like the modest, selfless princess she was, demurely replied:

> "I don't need anything."

Despite his devoted ministrations, Elena was growing weaker.

Taking her pulse I felt that it was weak, the breathing shallow, the general appearance anemic, and a certain debility indicating disturbed blood circulation. Knowing how easily she took offense I did not tell her that, apart from improper treatment, she had an abscess on her leg caused my so many injections by another doctor. Lest she should become overexcited, I spent only a few minutes in the house. Then, with a mixture of relief and sorrow, I left and spent the night with preparations for a determination campaign to save her life despite all obstacles.

Before I could start, new tests were needed. So the next day, I brought armsful of fruit and little delicacies, which, as I knew, would stimulate my girl's appetite. I was quite shocked to find how weak she had become. She only took a little fruit, for when her mother brought her a cup of good chicken broth, I noticed how Elena secretly emptied it out into the bucket near the bed.

He began his new series of treatments cautiously because he did not want to again alienate the family. To get them accustomed to the voltage, he first brought over a small "inductor box" powered by a dry-cell battery. It had a small movable shocking coil with silk cords and brass handles. With the handle, Elena could regulate the current which tickled and delighted her.

Thinking it was great fun, she exclaimed,

"Call Mama and Nana, Carl."

They all came and Elena played the joke on them and made Nana jump, and so she made her mother. Gradually the family, if it did not acquire much scientific knowledge of electricity, was at least convinced that it was fun and did no harm.

However, despite his attempts to brighten her mood, Elena's disease was obviously well advanced.

That evening, I noticed for the first time that Elena coughed quite severely, was short of breath, and had a sinking temperature.

Carl's plan was to attack the disease both medically and spiritually. Medically, the little electrical box he'd invented was a warm-up for the bigger and better high-power, high-frequency medical unit with a glass globe affixed to the top showing current.

Spiritually, he sought to elevate Elena's moods by giving her more presents. Nothing was too good for his Elena. When her rowdy family broke her bed by lounging around on it, Carl again came to the rescue.

> The following afternoon the furniture company delivered the bed, the best and biggest bed I had been able to find. Soon afterwards, there came another van with the largest mosquito top I had ordered and sheets of silk, cushions in pink and blue and the dresser. Well, my darling was as happy as a princess in the fortress of her big, new bed....
>
> "Don't forget that I want to marry you, darling," I said.

Perhaps we will share it someday, he thought. Once again, it was a prophecy that would, in a strange way, come to pass.

Elena loved the presents and the attention, yet she abhorred the shock therapy. The visits to her home were always the same—first the presents including wine and fruit, then the electrodes that von Cosel painstakingly put on her chest. The electricity that surged through her body literally jolted her until she cried out.

What Carl did to enable him to visit was buy his way back into Elena's life. In return, she allowed him to treat her, and, naturally, examine her chest as a doctor must. Electricity, the unlikely third corner of a love triangle, consummated the extraordinary attachment this physician had for his patient.

It was after one of the treatments that Carl, in his memoirs, claimed Elena initiated a wedding of sorts.

> "If I must die ... all I can leave you is my body. For I am only a sick girl, so I can't marry you while I am sick. But you will take care of my body after I am dead, won't you?"
>
> I promised I would and it was the most sacred promise which I ever made in life.
>
> I kissed her then and laid her gently back into her cushions and put her feet high so as to get blood circulation back

into her head, for her breath was getting short.
This was what I considered as our marriage vow.

A pivotal coincidence, at least in von Cosel's mind, occurred after the unusual ceremony described above, when Elena introduced him to one of her favorite songs. When the doctor entered her room, she was propped up in her new bed, browsing through a mail order catalog. As if by some preordained design, the song that was playing on the radio was "La Boda Negra," "The Black Wedding."

The beauty of the melody caught von Cosel's attention and she translated the story for him.

> *Oye, la historia que conto me un dia*
> *Un Viejo enterador de la comarca*
> Let me tell you all a story I was told
> By an undertaker of the region
> A young man's lover died before their wedding
> Without her love he simply could not reason

"At night he would visit the graveyard until he could stand it no longer," she explained. "Rescuing her from the grave, he placed her body on a bed of flowers, and then, before taking his own life, recited his weddings vows with his dead lover."

Al esqueleto regido abrasado—"her rigid skeleton he embraced."

"La Boda Negra," "The Black Wedding," the song enthralled him. And, after hearing it a second time, he considered this dark foreboding ode to death "their" song. Elena loved to sing and though she was weak, she could get through a couple of verses before running out of breath and closing her eyes.

Even when she rested, von Cosel's machines were on the job.

My own home-built million-volt equipment I was unable to use because it weighted tons and would have necessitated the laying of concrete foundations in Elena's house. The machine I had brought was a high-power, high-frequency medical unit with violet ray equipment, fulguration and throat examining attachments. It was strong enough to induce artificial fever.

This now I placed near her bed and plugged the connection into the light socket. I switched on the Tesla coil and hooked it up with one of the throat vacuum tubes.... I then asked her to open her mouth wide and to hold still while I slowly inserted the tip of the glass tube until it almost reached her tonsils. For a while she was very patient but when she became nervous, she moved a little which, of course, had the effect of a little hot bite from the frequency sparks on her tonsils and tongue. I withdrew the tube whenever this happened and I heard her pathetic little complaint:

"The electricity has bitten me...."

I left the spark discharge on the wide gap for another hour. In this manner, her room was charged with enough oxygen electrons for a whole night's sleep.

The next night, I applied five minute larynx radiation with the ultra-electrode tube to prevent dyspnea. Then, exchanging the electrode for a surface tube, I gave the outer surface of the throat and chest an all-over, high-frequency radiation for thirty minutes with medium strength. She enjoyed this as she would have a bath; it did her a lot of good because this radiation stimulates the tissues to new activity. Again, there was pronounced absence of coughing and her voice was stronger.

When Elena's condition improved slightly one day, the Count became more optimistic.

"I feel so much better, Carl," she said, "perhaps I can soon go out a little and my first trip will be to church."

To boost her spirits, Carl went to Holzberg's store and bought not one or two, but six silk dresses and also silk stockings.

But first, before any ventures out and about, she needed more electrical treatment.

I laid her on the autocondensation cushions and placed one sponge electrode on her chest, gradually increasing the high frequency current until the milliampere showed four hundred. I let it stay there and told her to cry out when it began to burn....

"Oh, Carl, it burns."

Then I gently reduced the flow of electricity to zero. Her body temperature had increased between one and two degrees above normal. The pain in the chest had disappeared, breathing was normal, but naturally pulse was fast. I covered her up with blankets and told her to rest. Again she was all right for the night.

Not only did Count von Cosel listen with Elena to "La Boda Negra" on the radio during his therapies, he was getting to hear more Spanish and Spanish songs than he could handle over the air waves and on the gramophone. The Latin spirit of "familia" and household filled with boisterous energy unnerved him.

All the more did it pain me to see her suffer, when a radio across the street was always being played full blast and father filled the house with all the Toms and Dicks and Harrys of the neighborhood who were noisy and forever nosy about the equipment around Elena's bed, crowding her and cheating her out of her last chance in life....

I had tested my own blood and found that it matched Elena's. I kept my equipment for blood transfusion in readiness and sterilized at all times. I was ready to give half of my own blood as a last resort.

To relieve her at least from the radio blare, I had my little organ moved over to her house. Now I sat down evenings and played some of the soft, old harmonies....

Wagner. He was one of the Count's favorites. The recurring theme of Wagner's *Parsifal* was that true love cannot exist on earth and that love in its most divine and complete form could take place only ... after death.

Von Cosel was said to have been an accomplished musician who could play the classics well. Predictably, he composed classics of his own dedicated to his deathly ill bride, and played them for her and other members of the staff at the Marine Hospital when the occasion arose.

As Elena's self-appointed guardian angel, he was ever vigilant in his efforts to maintain some sense of order and peacefulness through his demeanor and music. It was extremely trying to him that Elena's family was unable to accept his ministrations as they continually disrupted the spiritual atmosphere the Count was trying desperately to establish by bringing in obnoxious visitors.

If violent behavior on his part wouldn't have been upsetting to Elena, von Cosel claimed he would have thrown them all out by the scruffs of their necks.

It was particularly bad at mealtimes, when her father brought in some fat proprietor of a local bar who would keep on talking to Elena in rapid Spanish while she held her bowl of soup between her little hands and it was getting cold and her fingers cramped and she was too polite to eat. Only once after waiting twenty minutes did I muster the courage to say in plain English:

"Don't pay any attention to that fellow. Go right ahead, Elena, and eat your soup." She looked at me as if hypnotized and the fat man left in a rage. She ate the cold soup from the bowl.

The fascination of the barkeeper was that he flashed a loud diamond ring before Elena's eyes. In such matters, she reacted like a child admiring it, so the only way for me was to outshine this diamond. I had one just as big on my own hand, but never flashed it about. I put it on her hand next to her wedding ring.

"Would you like this one darling?"

She nodded.

"Here you are, darling, I give it to you with my love."

She blushed with joy.

"Look, mother, look here, now I have a real big diamond ring," she called happily, forgetting her misery for a time.

October 11, 1931, was the date Carl returned from the jewelers with the ring. Elena's condition on that hot, still summer day in the middle of hurricane season was sinking.

And so von Cosel was aghast when he learned that Elena's dad had taken her for a walk. He pleaded with her not to drain her strength, and admonished her because she might have collapsed in the middle of the road.

To her father, a little walk, some fresh air, an automobile ride, if she desired—could not be denied. She loved the cool breeze that blew her hair away from the back of her neck as she rode around town in a borrowed Ford Model T.

A few days later, October 16th, Carl was fuming when he found Elena had gone for another automobile ride with her father. In anger he carried her from the car, and placed her in the "Trendelingberg position" before begging her:

> "Get well and your airplane is waiting for you and we'll go together any place you like to see."

A final tug of war then broke out between von Cosel and Elena's father. The Count's intentions were good, but so were those of Elena's family. Both were certain they were doing the right thing. That Elena was going to die was inevitable from the day she contracted the horrible disease. From that moment on, it was only a question of when and what she would do in between. Her father, mother, sisters and relatives, knowing how ill she was, were doing what they thought was best for her. Except for the occasional outing, she spent most of her days in the small room decorated with a statue of St. Cecilia and a vase with a red rose.

By Friday, October 23rd, Elena was in a very exhausted state. Drifting in and out of consciousness, perspiring when the fever broke, struggling hard to get a breath, she appeared to be having a bad dream.

Irrationally, Von Cosel still clung to the delusion that there could be a cure and that, despite the extensive damage, the lesions would begin to heal again. He still thought radiation treatments would help.

> I had hopes that, despite the extensive damage, the lesions would heal again. I had hopes that, when Elena was out of danger, we would get married. As long as she lived I never abandoned hope.

Chapter Seven
The Parade on Duval Street

The first cold front of winter usually blows in by the end of October, and it's a welcome, invigorating change. The temperature dips into the low seventies, and everyone puts on winter clothes and jackets.

Duval Street was and still is the main street of Key West. Stretching two miles from the Atlantic Ocean to the Gulf of Mexico, it was the commercial and honky-tonk heartbeat of the town inhabited by some 11,000 residents. Even during Prohibition things could get lively on a Saturday night. The only difference that Prohibition made was that booze was sold from the back door rather than the front door and beer was hard to come by.

By October 20th of that year, people in town were getting ready for the Halloween parade on Duval Street, which would take place on Saturday, October 31st, Halloween night. Leading the parade would be the sheriff, followed by the Key West "Fighting Conchs" High School band. After they marched by, there would be a number of children dressed up as ghosts and goblins walking along. Bringing up the rear would be the conga line that went on until the parade sort of petered out about thirty minutes after it had begun. There's nothing quite like a small town parade, and the weather change made people feel refreshed as they helped the children get together their trick-or-treat costumes.

For one family though, the gaiety was false and the laughter contrived. Elena Hoyos was close to death and her friends and relatives knew that the end could come at any moment. Count von Cosel was aware of the dire seriousness of her condition but he would not permit himself to admit it. Still a dark reality cast its fatal shadow.

Sunday, October 25, 1931, I had just finished my records

after the day's work in the hospital and was about to put on my black coat which I always wore for my Sunday visit with my bright Elena, when the brakes on a car screeched in front of the laboratory door.

Mario, husband of Elena's sister Nana, rushed in and told me breathlessly:

"Elena has just died, come with me."

Now I knew the cause of the oppression which had gripped me all day long.

We raced through the town. It was just 5 p.m. when we reached her house. More than a block away, we could already hear the people moan and scream. There was a big crowd around the house; we had to break a passage through the people.

Hoping against hope that something could be done, I requested all the people to get out of the room. Then I went down on my knees before the bed, tested her breath and heartbeats. But there was nothing to be heard above the screams of the people. I placed the faradic testing electrode on her neck so that it covered the nerve region. There was no reaction. That moment Dr. Galey arrived. He, too, examined her to find that all life was gone.

Von Cosel's grief took the form of anger. He berated Mario for not coming earlier, then he blamed the family once again for the inevitable.

"If only you had come to me half an hour earlier, perhaps it wouldn't have been too late!"

"I drove as fast as I could," Mario mumbled. "What more could I do?"

He had lost time trying all doctors in town but found none at home.

In halting words, Mario told him what had happened. Despite repeated warnings, her father, again, had taken Elena on an automobile ride downtown. At least, according to von Cosel, it was a farewell befitting a Spanish Princess:

> She had dressed herself for the occasion in her new silk dress with all her jewelry and she waved to all the friends she had met in the streets. Nobody suspected that this was her last farewell.
>
> Though Elena was gone, the acrimony between him and the family continued.
>
> Elena's jaws had dropped but her eyes were bright and clear. They had a faraway look and as I gazed into those beloved eyes, they seemed to become deeper and deeper like wells, which, with magnetic power, drew me in. I could not tear my eyes away from her; I could look forever.
>
> With shock, I noticed that already she had been stripped of all the finery she had worn and that she was now clad in some cast-away and dirty old shirt which I had never seen before. Likewise, I noted that all the jewelry I had given her was gone.
>
> My poor darling Elena; with her body still warm, she had been robbed of everything she ever possessed on earth.

In his grief, von Cosel hated Elena's family because they hadn't followed his instructions about rest and visitation and because they had the audacity to repeatedly question his motives and abilities.

According to the Count, it was he who made and paid for the funeral, saving Elena from a disgraceful burial at the hands of her family. Elena's father, he claimed, introduced him to Mr. Pritchard, the funeral director, and pleaded with him to make the arrangements, which he did.

At the funeral home, von Cosel selected the coffin, the flowers, and made the decisions required for the final disposition of his beloved. He cowed a sobbing Nana into returning the silk dress and some of the jewelry she had taken "like a thief in the night," so that Elena would be viewed in something finer than the dirty rags she was wearing when he found her. He probably changed her dress himself. It wouldn't have been right for anyone else at the funeral home to see his wife/patient disrobed, and Nana couldn't be trusted.

The next day, October 26th edition of the *Key West Citizen* ran the obituary:

MISS ELAINE HOYOS, 22, DIED SUNDAY
AT 4:30 P.M.

Miss Elaine Hoyos, 22, died yesterday afternoon 4:30 o'clock at the residence 1228 Watson Street. Funeral services will be held this afternoon 5 o'clock from the residence to St. Mary's Star of the Sea Church, Rev. A.L. Maureau officiating. Pritchard's Funeral Home has charge of the arrangement.

Though grieving, Carl saw to each detail.

Throughout these technicalities, I wondered over the fact that I was able to calmly and deliberately arrange all these things. The strange part of it was that with my brain, I fully realized that Elena was dead but my heart, with a greater force told me: "She is not dead." It was probably because I listened to the voice of my heart much more than to that of my brain, that the brain was able to keep on functioning in a reasonable manner.

The funeral director was most courteous as he helped the Count make the most difficult decisions required for Elena's viewing.

"Doesn't she look lovely? She looks as though she's sleeping," the funeral director said softly, more as a compliment to himself than Elena. He couldn't help but think how much easier things were when they were young and died from natural causes.

> *Elena we will miss you*
> *Your laugh your gentle smile*
> *The love you gave to those around you*
> *Showed in your eyes dark as night*

Lying in a casket lined with rose-colored silk, the perfection of her features and the serenity of her expression calmed those who mourned and whispered, "It's such a shame, she was so young."

"Count von Cosel, I congratulate you for sparing no expense." The funeral director continued, "So often people don't realize that this is their final farewell to their loved one. It's sad when they try to save a few pennies here and a few pennies there during their last few precious moments. So often their selfishness haunts them for the rest of their lives. They feel their loved ones looking down from the heavens saying, "Wasn't I worth a comfortable casket to lie in for eternity? Wasn't I worth a few dozen roses?"

From the funeral home, the body in the casket was returned to Elena's home and the funeral was set for 5 p.m. on October 26, 1931.

Von Cosel, though beside himself with sorrow, worked all of that day. At four o'clock he closed his office, dressed, and went to the service.

> There was a surprisingly large number of mourners; masses of flowers formed almost a solid wall around my Elena's house.
>
> There was nobody in Elena's room. I took a seat near the coffin so I could drink in all her beauty for a last time. Beneath the closed lids, her eyeballs seemed to have concentrated and they were looking straight into my eyes; I could feel their stare like a hypnotic touch. I sat lonely at Elena's side among the flowers during this last hour.
>
> More and more people passed by the coffin depositing more flowers and the whole room now seemed filled with flowers and their overpowering fragrance. One thing which impressed me was the reverent silence of all these Latin peoples, who usually were so loud, being a Spanish custom. It was only I, however, who sensed Elena's spirit floating in the room....
>
> The undertaker awoke me from my reveries; the funeral procession was about to begin, and everybody had to take seats in the cars waiting outside....
>
> At the very last moment, when the coffin was about to be closed, and everybody was out of the room, I took a letter from my breast pocket and put it under Elena's dress on her breast. Then I kissed her good-bye on the temple which was the one place which had remained uncontaminated by other kisses.

> *The letter read:*
> *Key West, 26-10-31*
> *Elena, my darling Elena:*

My love for you is greater than ever. You are now free from all of your fetters, and you are free to go where you wish. Elena, please come to me, sweetheart. I long so much for you, tell me, what shall I do? As I cannot live without you, will you have me darling? Then take me or you come to me and stay with me until I can go with you, my sweetheart, Elena.

Your own Carl

It was a very long procession, one hundred cars, which followed my bride and me to her resting place. All along the way there sounded in my ears Beethoven's Seventh Symphony. Mad as this must appear to most people, to me this funeral procession was like a wedding march, and the slow stepping of pallbearers along the hearse in front of my car beating the proper measure for this symphony.

At church, the organ sounded with its angels' voices of a happy meeting in the better world. It was only then that I cried and cried from happiness. For now the long, sad, worldly struggle was all over. My bride was beyond malice, beyond unhappiness, beyond her pain. She was in the hands of God, the best, the gentlest hands that be.

It was highly doubtful there were a hundred cars. There may not have been that many on the entire island, but the funeral was well attended. The procession left the Star of the Sea Catholic Church and entered the cemetery at the Margaret Street gate, where the sexton's office was located. Slowly, slowly, they marched down the narrow cemetery road to the Catholic section. Wood folding chairs set in the grass facing the grave were there for the immediate family when they arrived. Above the hole that had been dug, the casket was suspended for yet another eulogy. A monsoon of tears fell from reddened eyes when the young and beautiful Elena was lowered into the ground.

The voyage of life is over
Your mortal afflictions past
No more pain and sorrow
Your spirit's free at last
Rest in Peace Elena

Funerals punctuate most deaths, placing for mourners a final and sad closure on the life of one they held dear. But this was not so for von Cosel.

> This then was what many, perhaps most people, would call "the end."
> A strange new kind of life now began for me. It was something like a rebirth after these last two oppressing and depressing years. Now at least nobody could take my Elena away from me. Although I could not see her any longer, I felt her presence all the time.
> It was only natural that I went daily to the cemetery. What disturbed me there was the fact that, owing to the nature of the ground, hers was a shallow grave and by no means safe from water.... There was no drainage of any kind in this cemetery.

The thirst the Count had for this lovely girl before death was never to be quenched. It was impossible for him to stop caring or to forget her even for a moment.

From his wingless airplane, the Count borrowed a tarpaulin which he placed over the tomb, securing it with stones. He rearranged the flowers and laid them on top of the tarp. Now it was time to get on with life but von Cosel couldn't.

Townspeople thought that his continual vigilance at the gravesite, now covered by the shielding tarp, was tragic but odd.

It was ... and it was only the beginning.

> Considering how often I have mentioned the strenuous relations between myself and Elena's family, readers will find it hard to understand why every night I went to her house.
> It was the memory, of course, which drew me there, the atmosphere of Elena lingering on. But that was exactly why I felt great sadness in finding her room desolate with all of Elena's things removed from it.
> When I inquired, the parents told me that everything was burned, and that they abhorred this house where one of theirs had died and that they were moving to some other part of town.

I had the distinct feeling that I was not being told the truth....

"Now, listen, if you are moving out, I'm going to rent this house for myself, even if I have to buy it. Moreover, you'd better be warned that the furniture and other things and jewelry I've given Elena were bought on the installment plan. If you want to keep these things for yourself, I will notify the company according to the contract and you have to pay the balance owing."

They did not like that particular idea....

No doubt they didn't. But, as Elena's heirs, they were legally entitled to her belongings. Their inheritance included, unconditionally, any gifts that had been given to her no matter who the source might have been or how much was owed by the giver. Von Cosel unwittingly bluffed them. In his heart and in his mind, he thought he was Elena's husband who should be first in line for the presents he had given her.

Friends of Elena, who talked to her daily when she was alive, have said that the jewelry was not very expensive. They couldn't remember the large diamond engagement ring von Cosel says he gave her, even though they were well aware of what the Count's latest gifts had been because Elena kept her friends abreast of his amorous offerings. In all fairness, the presents may not have been as extravagant as the Count describes them, but in 1931, with times as lean as they were, any jewelry was a luxurious gift.

Just as I had foreseen, the furniture was now produced from somewhere and placed back in Elena's room. Nothing had been burned except a few sheets and pillows, and the trunk which had been the family's.

Delighted with the result, I now told them:

"No matter whether you move or stay on, I'm going to live in my Elena's room, where she has lived and died because I distinctly feel at home in her presence."

To this they agreed and from then on I slept in Elena's bed. It still preserved the sweet scent of her hair...

It seems weird that her parents consented. But due to their sorrow, they most probably were confused and bereaved. Of course, poor as they were, they needed the five dollars a month in rent money he was going to pay them.

The new living arrangements led to at least one other worldly conversation:

> Regarding the jewels, Mother told me ... they were locked up.
>
> "Keep them," I told her, "until the tomb is ready. Then I'll adorn her with all her jewels, because I don't want anybody else to wear them."
>
> "Ah, but what's the use? There won't be anything left of Elena but bones," she said.
>
> "Don't you believe it, Mother. I'll take good care of her. I'll not permit her body to decay, and if in the grave Elena should lose her hair, I'll buy new hair and put it back on her head."
>
> "Don't do that," said the mother, "don't use other people's hair, put her own back—I have some which she cut off a year ago."
>
> At these words, she opened her dresser and took out ... the beautiful long tresses of my Elena which had been cut off a year ago when she decided to wear her hair in the American style. This package she gave me, for which I thanked her with all my heart.
>
> Having resigned herself to all my determination, Mother was now a very much changed woman indeed, and in a way so was the father too. Both were satisfied that I would take care of Elena and were convinced of my undying love for her.

The tarpaulin the Count had placed covering Elena's tomb protected her beautiful form from the torrential rain, but this was only a temporary solution to the long-term decay problem the Count promised to forestall.

> I disconnected the radio in my room which I had purchased for Elena, that from now on was to be silent as a tribute to her death.

It was the same radio on which Elena and the Count together had listened to "their" song, "La Boda Negra."

> *At night he would visit the grave yard*
> *And dream about the days she was alive*
> *His tears would fall upon her tombstone*
> *The tombstone of the girl to be his bride*

From the moment Count Carl von Cosel fell for Elena, he was perpetually doing something for her—making autocondenser cushions, building high-voltage machines to heal her, taking her gifts, even buying her the mahogany bed.

Now that she was dead and buried there was nothing else for him to do except worry about how to protect her "beautiful form." But what should he do? How could he care for her below the ground? In a moment of inspiration, he realized that it was his duty to erect a grand mausoleum both as a testament of his love and a way to remove her from the grave.

An architectural monument to his Elena was the next step.

Chapter Eight

The Mausoleum and the Great Escape

In Elena's former bedroom, sleeping on the bed he had given her, the Count was able to rest more peacefully than he had for some time.

During the day, he still worked at the hospital. The rest of the time he spent designing and constructing the new mausoleum.

> I bought a larger plot around Elena's grave, sufficient for a family tomb. There I sat every afternoon after work on a little chair, drawing plans and waiting for the mason who had promised to help me with the work.... Meantime, the first heavy rains drenched the cemetery and I became very much concerned over my Elena, especially since I suspected odor developing from the shallow grave.

Because von Cosel planned to build the ornate crypt over the plot where Elena was buried, he had to get a disinterment permit to remove her body from her underground grave. With the Hoyos family and the state of Florida's permission, Elena made her second trip to a funeral home. She would eventually make three. This time it was Lopez Funeral Home that stored her body while von Cosel went forward with not one, but two tasks he felt he had to accomplish. First, he had to construct Elena's new and improved home in the Key West Cemetery. Second, von Cosel thought it was imperative that he, secretly, "re-bed" her body just in case there had been water damage—he wanted to see her again.

To build the crypt he had designed, he had to purchase an additional plot adjacent to the one where she was resting. Then, he found a mason. The construction took three months, one for the actual construction, one to let the cement cure, and one to finish the interior.

The re-bedding of Elena was an extremely unorthodox and un-heard-of procedure, so it had to be done surreptitiously in the mid-dle of the night. Perhaps a little money to the undertaker on the side helped von Cosel gain access to the morgue and the key to Elena's vault.

Surely, the family had no idea what the Count was secretly doing inside the funeral home, despite the fact that they were living under the same roof and could hear him leaving and coming at all hours. Under artificial light in the bowels of the funeral home, von Cosel, perhaps with Wagner playing in his mind, rendezvoused with his dead love.

> Disinterment revealed that rains had indeed soaked the coffin and that moreover it had been partially crushed when a couple of grave diggers had trampled down the ground too hard after the funeral. It was with dire anticipation that I now approached the urgent task of taking Elena out of the dam-aged coffin and placing her into a new and stronger casket I had bought.
>
> Toward this purpose, the mortician and I arranged it so that there were no other dead in the morgue at the date for the re-bedding of her body. In preparation, I had bought all that could possibly be needed; new sheets, pillow, sterile cot-ton, gauze, chemicals, and sprays. I also built in my spare time an incubation tank and had placed it in the morgue just in case it should be needed.
>
> This done, I took a taxi and hastened to Elena's house to fetch her jewels which now were to be restored to her. Mother raised no difficulty over this; she gladly handed me the little box filled with the glittery toys and I hastened back.

If von Cosel was squeamish as he opened the casket and began the re-bedding, he never let on.

> After all the customary sanitary precautions had been taken, I opened the seals of the vault for which I had a key. The inner coffin, much damaged, became visible. Together we slid it out and set it on the concrete floor.

The opening of the lid gave us considerable trouble, owing to the demolished boards lying inside on the body and because its lining inside had become attached to Elena's face and body. The contents were now laid bare.

As the first step, I sprayed diluted formalin all over the shrouded body in ample quantities. This was for disinfection and also to harden the body tissues before we undertook to detach from the skin the drapery which had become glued to it.

Decay had set in a most disheartening manner. Only with the greatest care was I able to peel the pieces of textile from the body; this took hours. We then lifted the body out of the coffin and laid it on a table on a clean sheet. Having sprayed the body all over again, I now proceeded to sponge her face with a specially prepared solution and also her hands and feet. With dismay, I discovered that in view of the damage already done, much more cleaning was required than could be done in the one night I had the morgue at my disposal.

Till dawn I worked with every energy, appalled at the negligence of the mortician who had failed to embalm the coffin which smelled awful, not the body.

When morning came, my sweet bride was free from all outward signs of decay and from that of odor. When the mortician came to work, we placed her on thick layers of cotton and after I sprayed her form all over with Eau de Cologne, we now covered it all around with similar layers of sterile cotton. This done, we lifted her into her new coffin, and then the coffin into the new metal outer coffin I had selected. This one I sealed all around with screws. The casket was of the air-tight type held together by a hundred screws.

Although the state court allowed the disinterment, it certainly had no idea what the Count and his accomplice were doing to Elena Hoyos's corpse in the dead of night. How one embalms a coffin was left unanswered.

If the mortician was nervous the first time, he was even more nervous when von Cosel informed the man that the Count would need yet another night, alone, in the embalming room.

A few nights thereafter, when I could again have the use

> of the morgue, I took Elena out of the inner coffin and placed her into my specially made incubator tank. After this had been completely sealed, a task which took till midnight, I poured into the top valve of the tank a certain solution which I had prepared for her, both antiseptic and nourishing for body cells. This I kept pouring until the tank was completely filled. The tank was then placed into the casket. Now I felt easier; at least for the time being Elena was protected against further decay.

Though von Cosel sometimes tailored the truth, the descriptions of his love for Elena, without a doubt, came from the heart; the descriptions of the scientific procedures he used to preserve Elena were, most probably, fact, not fiction.

Essentially, von Cosel submerged Elena's body in a homemade "incubator tank," similar to suspending objects in formaldehyde.

Later, Elena was placed in a double casket and, according to the Count, this was special and made-to-order.

The inner casket lid was fastened with a hundred screws and fitted with two valves—one for filling and one for draining. The outer casket, made of steel, was secured by more than fifty locks that required a key.

When the mausoleum was finally finished:

> It looked more like a pleasant summer residence than a burial place, and that it really was for my dear bride. This is exactly what I desired for her and I felt sure she would like this, her new little house. Onlookers passing by said they would like to move in it and make it their house.

It was now time to place Elena there.

> The night before she was to move to her new residence, I wrote a certain letter and in the morning took it with me to the tomb. The undertaker did the placement of the casket and then he left me, and I laid down the crucifix on top of it and lighted the little votive lights in the niche above her head, lights which from now on were to burn there day and night.
>
> This done, I closed the little curtains of blue silk which

were to prevent curious people from peeping in, and saying good-bye to my bride for today I left her little house, carefully locking its door with three locks.

The Key West Cemetery wasn't nearly so crowded as it is today. In 1940, most of the existing tombs were widely spaced family plots with elaborate iron or cement fences surrounding them. But, as intricate as they were, Elena's "little house" was the Taj Mahal of the Catholic section. Less than a hundred feet from Frances Street, surrounded by palm and pine trees, it was a unique structure with an ornate cement dome supported by Greek pillars. A cross adorned the top. Inscribed in the rectangle marble headstone embedded in the cement wall next to the entrance was:

Elena Milagro Hoyos
born July 31-1909.
died October 25-1931.
R.I.P.
Ct. d. Cosel.

On either side of the entrance there were pedestals for vases of flowers. On the four corners of the mausoleum, von Cosel placed large cement urns that he had himself made for planting flowers. The short, wide doors had a glass window and curtains. A white porcelain door knob contrasted with the dark plate surrounding it.

The eye von Cosel carved about Elena's name on the expensive marble plaque seemed wide awake, looking out for her in her slumber. The "Ct. d Cosel" inscribed in the lower right hand corner is very curious. If he were merely signing the headstone, wouldn't he have inscribed, "Ct. von Cosel"? He offers no explanation in the memoirs, but it's possible that this was his obscure way of telling the world that Elena was now his wife—Countess damsel Cosel. This could have been his attempt at giving Elena his own last name, since he had no intention of including her married name, "Mesa" on the inscription.

The Latin inscription on the base of the dome read poetically: *"Accersitus ab Angelus"*—"Summoned by Angels."

Von Cosel, walking to and from the tomb with his ornate cane or umbrella, became a familiar sight to those living nearby. He was so proud of what he had done for his beloved bride, Elena. The mausoleum was in a beautiful grassy part of the cemetery which was used like a park back then. Families would bring a picnic lunch and join their departed under a blooming poinciana tree for a couple of hours while the children played hide-in-seek among the tombstones. With the sky clear blue, the tall palm trees looked as if they reached all the way to heaven.

> Every evening I went to the little house I had built for her. I didn't do this from a plan or with any specific intention. I just felt drawn to the spot by some magnetic power which always increased toward evening and became quite irresistible when the sun set below the horizon. There were days when I had no intention whatsoever to go, when indeed I had pressing work on my hands. Each time, however, I simply had to drop everything for the rendezvous. The moment I reached the cemetery, I always experienced a sudden relief from the urge, the pressure which had driven me. I had indeed a date, I felt it.

But now that this big undertaking was completed, von Cosel was again left with nothing to do for his Elena. He sat alone in the crypt where:

> The troubled past reappeared before the mind's eye like a motion picture reel. At times I felt very tired in the consideration of this past, and then it happened and I fell asleep.

For eighteen months, von Cosel came faithfully to the tomb, sitting inside on a small chair near the coffin, brooding.

> It had been a sultry day and I had left the door wide open so that the refreshing coolness of the night could enter. The moist heat, however, was still in the room and this was probably the reason I fell asleep. Suddenly I was aroused by a loud, crashing report as if a cannon had been fired close to my ear. Thus roughly awakened I thought for a moment that perhaps some mischievous kid had fired a toy pistol to frighten me. But there was nobody around ... I noticed by the reflection

of the street lights outside that fifty locks which held the metal casket had sprung open. I examined them closely and it was perfectly clear that they had been sprung with great force and all at once, and that this must have been the loud report which had aroused me.

Standing there in the semi-darkness I smiled. … I remembered how fond Elena always had been of the fun of a practical joke. This breaking of the locks looked very much like Elena to me; perhaps she thought it funny to jolt her bridegroom in this manner who had dared to fall asleep in her presence.

Now I could clearly hear a tapping or crackling sound inside, very distant, like nails of delicate fingers, probing and scratching a metal surface.

With spontaneous resolution, I got the keys of out my pocket and quickly opened the remaining locks of the casket, and with some effort I succeeded in lifting the heavy lid. Starlight revealed that the inner coffin was still intact and sealed….

I bent my ear to the inner coffin and listened intently. There was no sound, and I removed its lid altogether… After screwing off the caps, I tested the top valve of the incubator, which had a filter of sterile cotton. As I took this filter out, a strange and pleasant perfume emanated and spread all over the room. There was no pressure of gas inside. There was only this mysterious smell which resembled hamine (fragrant chemical in human blood) and not any manufactured perfume. It was exactly like the healthy and agreeable odor of a young woman's skin on a warm day. It simply was the typical odor which I loved so much of my bride, Elena, and of her hair.

Thereafter, he began striking up conversations with Elena. As her faithful lover and everlasting suitor, he came to see her almost every night.

After a while I placed my ear against the open valve and after a minute or so I heard her voice. Very distinctly, in soft tones; it sounded so very much alive that I instinctively looked around everywhere to see whether, by any chance, she was standing somewhere nearby....

From that day on, he was sure. Elena was there with him.

> I brought her flowers every night and other presents too.... One day it would be a few pretty handkerchiefs, the next a Spanish shawl, a comb, a vanity case. My greeting cards were always:
> "God bless you, darling. I am so happy to be with you."
> If this appears a strange or crazy thing to do, let me repeat, that once in India I had lain for dead myself and had thought I still were in my bed, whereas in reality, I had already been placed into the morgue. From this, my own case, and from many others on record, I knew that death is not the end of life and the resurrection from the grave is actually a possibility.

At this point, von Cosel felt he was communicating with Elena's spirit and that she spoke to him.

> A curious fact was that Elena's spirit showed all the curiosity of a very young girl, a curiosity which extended to the contents of my pockets. Sometimes I carried things from the hardware store which I need for my plane. Invariably, Elena would ask me:
> "What is in that paper bag in your right coat pocket?"
> And I would laughingly explain:
> "Oh, darling, those are screws and little brass nails I need for your plane."
> Often she was not satisfied with the explanation unless I spread the screws and nails, or whatever it was, on top of the coffin for her to see.

Anyone walking down Frances Street by the cemetery, close to the mausoleum, surely quickened his step when, on a dark night, he heard the laughter and the talk of the Count echoing off the cement walls inside the tomb of the dead Elena.

She insisted on all amenities of polite conversation. I never failed to greet her and say good-bye in the ceremonious, Spanish manner....

One Christmas afternoon, I had come earlier than my usual hour in order to take a photograph of the tomb. Later, when it had become dark and I was sitting inside, all of a sudden I felt hands feeling all over my face and head. I could not see anything, but the touch was the familiar one of Elena's. That night at home I developed the picture I had taken. I had taken thousands of pictures with this self-same camera and it had never failed. This picture, however, showed a white shape, resembling a human figure as if outlined in a bright white light, standing at the entrance of the tomb.

The constant nagging of the curious had irritated me so much that I changed my visiting hours further into the night. It was the time of the full moon and the cemetery was almost as brightly lit as in the daytime, so it could not have been that my eyes deceived me when on my next visit I saw a veiled, white figure at the entrance to the tomb.

As I came near, it started moving as if it had been waiting for me. I hastened to meet her but when I was only a few yards away, she disappeared through the locked door.

Inside the tomb ... the pleasing smell which emanated from the valve was particularly strong that night. As I always did, I held my hands over the valve into this beloved odor of my beautiful bride, Elena. It was remarkable how long this odor clung to my hands; even washing would not remove it.

Within the week the moon was waning fast, the nights became darker, and by the end of the week, only a narrow sickle of the moon was left.

Ever since the moon began to wane, Elena had begun to sing in her casket with a very soft, clear voice which became a little stronger from night to night. It was always the same old Spanish song about a lover who opens the grave of his dead bride. I could distinctly hear and understand every word.

If he could imagine Elena speaking, he could also hear her beautiful voice singing. She loved to sing—*Accersitus ab Angelus,* she was singing with the angels. Over and over again, she sang the lyrics of the song she had sung to him before her death. Wasn't "their" song telling him to plan his own black wedding? Wasn't Elena crying out from the tomb, begging him to take her home with him?

> *On a night when thunder roared and lightning flashed*
> *He broke apart the tombstone of her grave*
> *With his hands he dug into the earth*
> *And in his arms he carried her away*

"**Dear Elena, everyone thought it was the end, didn't they? We knew, didn't we, that it was only the beginning. Now, in death, no one can take you from me. I know how relieved you were when I removed your coffin from the ground. I knew you weren't safe from the torrential rains. I couldn't stand to have your beautiful form perish from the ground water.**

"**It's hard to believe that I have been visiting you here for almost two years. When I put my hands on your casket it always feels warm. It feels as though electricity is passing through my arms. Do you like this little house I built for you?**"

The rumble of distant thunder was a fitting percussive note for what was about to transpire.

"Do you love me, Carlos?"

Putting his mouth to the valve, he replied,

"Elena! Why would you say such a thing?"

"You do still love me, don't you, Carlos?"

"Of course I love you. Why would I visit you night after night?"

"Tell me then, Carlos, am I really dead?"

"No, Elena, you are not dead. Your body is asleep. Your spirit is dreaming."

"Carlos, where do I live?" (Thunder!)

"You live in the little house I built for you. I built it to protect you. I wanted you to be safe."

"Is this your house, too?"

"No, Elena, I come here to visit you." (Thunder/crash!)

"Carlos, listen to me. I want to go home with you. I want to be with you."

After a while, haltingly, but firmly, came her voice again:
"Carlos, don't you listen to the words of the song I sing to you
every time you visit? It's the same song I used to sing before I died;
the one we heard together on the radio during my treatments—'La
Boda Negra,' 'The Black Wedding.' Don't you know why I sing to
you 'our' song?

"But Elena, there are problems:"

> You see, this cemetery is surrounded by streets and
> houses. It has several gates, but they are all in full view of the
> houses, and automobiles are passing back and forth past the
> cemetery at all hours. People are curious. They are quite used
> to seeing coffins go into the cemetery, but they have never
> seen the dead come out again. If they see us, people might
> raise hell. What are we going to do about this, darling?"

Elena had a plan for the skeptical Count:

> "Go out in front of the tomb, Carlos, and I will show you
> how this can be done."
> Now standing in front of the tomb, I viewed with great
> misgivings the scenery around … the tomb….
> "You do it this way; when the moon changes, you bring
> along a very large blanket. You hang that blanket over the rail
> of the fence. Then nobody can see you from the street or from
> the houses, Carlos. The woman, my neighbor in the grave,
> she is my friend. She will be glad to help you."
> Unmistakably Elena's spirit now used the full extent of its
> power over my nervous system. She directed my every step;
> I merely acted like a radio receiver to the waves which came
> from her.

But first, before von Cosel did the infamously legendary deed that
would forever make him a part of Key West history, there had to be
a dress rehearsal.

> This rehearsal of the drama in which I had to be an actor
> the following night was so perfect that it seemed to me as if
> the coffin were already following me. I just listened to her

voice which guided me, which directed me in every turn so cleverly that I was always kept out of sight from the houses and from the road....

I was prepared to risk my life, and to face any danger which would cross my path this night. There was no half way, this was clear to me. Once it was started it had to be carried out to a finish. This was my resolve. Besides, I did not know of a single person whom I could trust who would be reliably discreet. And she would have to come out, if ever I was to take proper care of her.

It was a mystical night for Count Carl von Cosel. He double-checked everything before taking the wagon, blanket, cushions, and rope down the stairs of the mausoleum. A black crucifix above Elena's coffin inexplicably glowed with a soft light as the Count extracted the inner casket from the outer one. This could not have been easy because they were so heavy.

At last the new moon had come. The night was pitch dark, and promises to the dead are scared and must be kept....

Leaving the door wide open, I went down inside and spoke a few words into the coffin valve.

"Darling, I have come to fulfill my promise to you. Sleep now, darling, gently for a while, until you are with me. God bless you."

He then loaded his darling bride onto the little wagon he had purchased and placed rubber cushions on either end. The blanket with the crucifix on top was tied around the casket with rope. Satisfied there was no one watching, he pulled the wagon from within the mausoleum. Their remarkable journey had begun:

A wonderfully elated feeling took complete possession of my entire being, as though a second spirit had entered my soul. It seemed that a bodyguard of veiled angels had formed on both sides and were coming along with us and a great inspiration filled me then. It made me feel like a victor, holding the triumphal entry in a world forgotten and buried. I felt secure, protected, and invulnerable. No matter what was coming against us now, nothing could harm either of us any more.

There was no place for the living here on this blackest of nights.

All of the cemetery was alive with souls which came out of the graves from all sides, moving and thronging all around us. It was indeed like a festival among the departed, as they moved up on all sides. It was like a great divine wedding march for me, taking place. It could not be a funeral march, for all seemed happy and joyful and interested in silent admiration, watching as the white forms of angels filed past with Elena and me in their midst. They were everywhere, none blocking our way, but all of them melting out of our way. It seemed as if they had never seen such a celebration in this cemetery before. It was as if all were delighted and desirous to help us. The little cart, for all of its weight, seemed almost to run by itself. It responded to the slightest touch of my hand, which gave me the impression of being aided on by friendly hands, reaching out of the ground.

Von Cosel's spirit soared until disaster struck. As he struggled to get the coffin over the cemetery fence, the ground collapsed under him and the whole load fell on top of him, squashing his new black felt hat. Summoning all of his strength and asking for divine help, he was able to lift the casket over the fence.

What was dripping on him? What was that running down his neck onto the satin lapels of his wedding jacket with an odor so foul the neighborhood dogs started barking? He hadn't planned on this during dress rehearsal.

With super-human effort, he was able to get the casket to the shed he had rented as a halfway house. He closed the leaky casket valve and pulled off all of his clothes. Since there was no running water, he had to wash himself and his clothes with a bottle of whisky he found on a shelf.

Still smelling strong, but more like liquor now, I closed up the house and went home by a long roundabout way, so as to give the wind and air a chance to take away the odor and dry my clothes.

It was a pitiful conclusion to the perfect escape.

Stoically, Count Carl von Cosel afterward walked the dark streets of Key West in his soiled wedding tuxedo, wearing his crushed new felt fedora, trying to figure out how to get into the house of Elena's parents without waking anyone. Once inside, he snuck into the bathroom reeking so badly that even bathing wouldn't get rid of the odor.

The following day, he decided to leave the coffin "at rest."

But the day after, seemingly undaunted—"promises to the dead are sacred"—he took Elena from the halfway house and loaded her into a large sedan.

> **Everything went fine; I arrived at the hospital grounds where the plane was without incident. This part of the hospital grounds, being behind the morgue, was quite deserted evenings. Undisturbed, I had now moved my beloved into the cabin of the plane. She now had taken full possession of it.**

"Come fly with me and be my wife, my heart thy resting place will be," an old German song Carl Tanzler's mother used to sing to him, played over and over in his mind as he stood back and looked at his wonderful airship which now held his wonderful bride. Von Cosel put his hands together and pulled them to his chest....

There was so much more that had to be done!

Chapter Nine
Life, Death and Airships

Von Cosel had kept his promise:

> Her wish had been fulfilled, and as Easter was close at
> hand, I made everything nice and cozy in her cabin. Her gar-
> ments, bridal dress, veil, flowers, and jewels, shoes, stockings,
> everything was at hand, with plenty of money, too. Gently, I
> slid the coffin aft from the pilot cabin into hers beneath the
> little curtained windows, which were all screened against in-
> sects. There was a tank of distilled water inside for washing
> and drinking, plenty of clean linen, and sterile cotton. Every-
> thing medical had been provided for, including a Carrel-
> Dakin instillation apparatus with solutions and chemicals.
> Her cabin was really the hospital of the ship.

The only time it was safe for von Cosel to work on his slumbering
love was in the dead of night when prying eyes would also be closed
in sleep. The first light of day was approaching as he finished removing the last of the one hundred screws securing the casket lid.
The "Carrel-Dakin instillation apparatus with chemicals and solutions" von Cosel readied for Elena actually was used during World
War I to treat infected wounds by irrigating them with antiseptics.

The next night, after snapping the latch of the door lock and locking himself in, he removed the final four screws and lifted the cover.

> I can hardly describe the picture which unfolded before
> my eyes. It was a horrible and a saddening sight to look inside
> the coffin after eighteen months in the grave. It was disheart-
> ening.
> "My poor darling, how you have been neglected. Of

course you could not help yourself and no one came to your aid. May God forgive me if I could not come to your aid in time to save you earlier. In your plight, your beautiful eyes broke and sank without anyone coming to bring you help. Your beautiful dress, it had decayed and now mars your beauty."

My very soul was tortured when I saw her awful condition. I resolved that I would help her out of this awful mess at once. She was my beloved bride; my promise to take care of her was a sacred one.

With the greatest of care, I now detached the uppermost layers [of clothing], which were overgrown and eaten up with slimy moulds. I then got a large bucket and deposited rags into it until it was filled. Careful peeling of all pieces around the head, face, and chest first, I found many pieces had become glued to the skin. All of those which did not come off easily, I left on her body to soak for the time being, as it might injure her delicate skin, which I wanted to keep intact. The bucket was heaping full and heavy. It had to be removed quickly as the odor was overpowering.

The fresh salt air that greeted him as he opened the door of the airship gave him a needed boost. Walking, almost running, he lugged the nauseating bucket two-hundred feet to the breakwater and dumped the organic mess into the ocean. Although discouraged again, he resolved to help Elena.

Then I prepared some soap solution and wetted all places and surfaces where rags were adhering to her body. Little by little the pieces loosened and came off, but not all of them that first night. Again and again I washed her body, tilting it carefully, first on one side, then on the other, so as to wash the back and remove the rags from underneath.... The bucket filled up once more and had to be taken out....

I rinsed her body and also inside the coffin thoroughly, but I used a phenol solution this time for disinfecting and to remove the last traces of odor. After that, I dried her entire body, drained the coffin and sponged it thoroughly.

The Count always amused Mrs. Weekley of Fausto's Food Palace when he came in to buy supplies. What could he be doing with all of the soap he was buying, six or more bars daily? And the perfume, what in the world was he doing with all of the Eau de Cologne? She thought he was a strange little man, and she was right.

Mrs. Weekley was not alone in thinking von Cosel was eccentric. He was suddenly awfully busy.

> I could find a little time to rest, to examine her body, and study its condition more thoroughly. I looked into the deep fallen cavities of the eyes, like deep, empty black holes, I saw her dried up lips, slightly parted with her white teeth gleaming between them. And when looking so long and deep into those black openings, where once her beautiful eyes shone so bright, it was strange indeed; it seemed as if a pair of pupils were forming again, deep inside, and were looking at me as from the bottom of a well, straight and seriously.

It was the eyes, windows to the soul, which bothered him most. He had to find a way to replace them.

As an employee at the medical facility, he had access to catalogues and was familiar with medical supply salesmen. The delicate part of his quest would be arranging the purchase of both a left and a right glass eye without arousing suspicion. Not that anyone would suspect that he had taken a woman, dead for two years from a grave; propriety was still in order. He couldn't go up to a salesperson and ask if he could buy a couple of eyes—brown, please, one left and one right. No, he probably ordered them from a mail order catalog and had them shipped—"attention Dr. von Cosel"—to the hospital.

Despite the condition of Elena's body, to him, it was sacred:

> My angel was pure, despite the mud and slimy rags in which she had been lying for so many months….
> And then I heard a soft voice speak into my ear:
> "Now you will love me no more, will you?"
> These words cut into my heart. Like an arrow, they set me on fire with sacred love for her. I assured her:
> "Darling, I love you more than ever before. If it were not

so, I would not have taken you to me."

Then kissing her dry lips, and breathing deeply into her lungs until her bosom rose, I unpacked her bridal gown and covered her body with it. I draped her with the silk veil and adorned her head and hair with a golden crown. She looked so wonderful now, I could not resist the wondrous spell and trembling with burning love, I sank gently into the coffin with her and kissed her as if she were alive.

Long I lay thus, holding her closely to me, the living and the dead united in love. The sweetness of this was divine. Never had I dreamt that she had preserved so sweet and intense a love for me after being in the grave for so long. Was it possible? I could hardly grasp or believe it, but there was the undeniable evidence. Life and death united together, eye to eye. Long and silent we lay. We needed no words. Words could not express the heavenly bliss that we were experiencing. We were two kindred spirits flowing together. It was soul resting within soul. It was sweet and lovely beyond human words or understanding. God bless her soul and body.

Outside the night passed into dawn and still I held her head and body embraced. It was hard to tear myself from this wonderful heavenly spell. At last I raised myself and laid her on the cushions, promising to come back by night. Then covering her up and lowering the lid carefully, without fastening it, I went home.

Ach wie ist's moglich dann, dass ich Dach lassen kann—How can I part from Thee? How can I leave Thee? I will not; I cannot Elena. He barely had time for a badly needed bath before he was due back at the hospital.

"Please forgive me, darling," I prayed. "You are an angel in death, you are purer than many a living."

Von Cosel, in his mysterious past, had studied the Hindu religion because he believed in Brahman wisdom. A Brahman is a member of the priestly Hindu caste, and Brahman is defined by Webster's Dictionary as "the supreme and eternal essence or spirit of the universe." Von Cosel's interpretation of the Brahman recipe for any in-

curable disease was to die and remain buried for one year; thereafter, you are cured. Von Cosel admitted that there were a few problems:

The first problem: few wanted to try it.

The second problem: the chemicals and "destructive agencies"
used by the embalmers preclude any possibility of coming back
again.

Another problem: since there is only one chance to come back
from the dead, when the body dies the second time, you are dead
forever. For this reason, the initial comeback must be handled with
delicacy and caution.

> Life is indeed a battle. This statement is in order, as really
> we fight from beginning to end, until, one by one, we drop
> out of combat. This may be only for a spell, unless some 'well-
> meaning' creature cuts and demolishes our vital organs in
> the meantime before we have a chance to recover. If only rel-
> atives and undertakers would act with more consideration
> for the dead. It is safe to estimate that many thousands of un-
> fortunates have been killed in the past by postmortem, em-
> balming, and too hasty burials. Modern science has advanced
> far enough to prove that death is not always final. In reality,
> death is just the first severe shock. Real or final death may
> follow, but not invariably.... It would be desirable to give the
> dead a chance instead of depriving them of the last chance
> that God has given them. It is a fact, mostly forgotten in the
> hustle of this modern life, that thousands of certified dead
> have recovered from the grave. Thousands lying in graves
> would still be alive if humanity had more sense and tolerance.

Von Cosel's beliefs were the reason he gave Elena's original em-
balmer detailed instructions on how to prepare her body, according
to the memoirs. Otherwise, the undertaker could have botched
Elena's second and last chance at life.

> The body reactions do not come as rapidly as before
> death, owing to deficient motor nerves. Still, the answer
> comes; slowly of course, because the body stands under the
> law of eternity for which a year of our lives may be no more

than a second.

Von Cosel felt in himself a state of heightened awareness, where he could comprehend and appreciate the slow-motion world of those on the other side. The fog that had initially prohibited him from seeing great truths had, in his mind, lifted enough so that he was beginning to transcendentally eclipse mere mortals who were still looking at their watches, not realizing that their lives were not more than a grain of sand on the beach of time.

> It was the Easter morn of 1933. It was her resurrection indeed when divine love had gently lifted my bride from the grave.

Cards and letters arriving from his wife, Doris Tanzler, were tossed aside. He had no time for them; his only thoughts were of Elena.

> How sweet she still was, even though some of the ravages of eighteen months in the grave had not yet been removed. I washed her frequently with perfumed soap and spirits of wine, and Eau de Cologne, still loosening many bits of clothing from her body....

Slowly and painstakingly, he attended to her. Nothing disgusted or repelled him in his efforts to bring her back to life.

> Her beautiful hair also needed plenty of washing, as it was still partly glued together and to her scalp. By further examination, I was not surprised to discover small maggots of the gnat-larvae type which were feeding on blood around her head and ears and on the surface of her abdomen.... I treated [the abdomen] with healing lotions and sterile packing, just like living tissue. I also bandaged up toes, feet, and fingers as they had badly suffered in the soil and threatened disintegration. I moistened these bandages with formalin to arrest further decay for the present.... There was no putrification anywhere on the body, although parts of it showed indication of losing binding element tissue.... Of course, I avoided any

corrosives, alum, and other mordants on her. Instead, I prepared solutions of a nourishing character with ingredients
like olive oil or glycerine and others I wish to keep secret.

The idea of awakening her in this condition was out of the
question....

Youthful as she was, full of life, there was no fast dying of
the forces of life, and with a little assistance, they will re-
cover....

Though the time was wrong for resurrection, he began making
some cosmetic improvements that would lead to a remarkable
transformation.

First, he put splints on Elena's nose that were kept in place with
bandages. They remained there for one month after which her nose
looked "as beautiful as when she was alive." Next, he had to
straighten out her arm which had been folded across her body in
the coffin. This he accomplished by counterweight with a cord over
a pulley on the ceiling, fastened to a bandage on the wrist. It applied
gentle tension until the arm automatically took the required position below the hip joint.

Hot solutions were then administered to restore her intestinal
tract.

But it was von Cosel's ability to make death masks that transformed Elena in a curious, unexpected, and significant way. Want-
ing to make a plaster cast of her so he would have a permanent,
nonperishable record of her face, he made several in hopes that one
would be absolutely perfect. Creating the masks, he incidentally discovered that the fine oiled silk which he had used to cover and protect her face, eyes, and hair, had fastened itself tightly to her skin.

Later, after incubation of her body, I had to extend the
same protection all over her body; only in this way was it possible to completely free her from those pests, which always
doggedly found a way to attack her and cheat my rigid pre-
cautions.

Though Elena was becoming a mummy, to von Cosel, she was returning to life.

Her hair, which had been flat and lifeless in her coffin, had become alive again, taking its own characteristic waves and curls. Her hair even regained its electrical properties; being attracted to my hands when they came near it. No matter what the cause, it indicated life, though different than before.

Elena's day-to-day existence with Carl, her doctor/husband soon took on a pattern of regularity.

Weeks and months passed. With the same routine of feeding and instilling vitamins into her body, she improved daily and even her living expression returned.

In the meantime, changes at the Marine Hospital were about to unsettle Carl von Cosel's everyday existence. The commander of the Naval Station of which the hospital was a part, died. His successor was much younger and refused to allow von Cosel to continue storing his airship on government property.

As orderly as the Count thought he was, he was not at all neat. The new chief was probably amazed that this unkempt area was allowed to exist in the first place. For things to be shipshape, the plane would have to be moved and soon. Fortuitously, a place where he could "build" his residence and airplane hanger was offered to von Cosel on Rest Beach.

Also, now that Elena was with him, there was no need for him to live with her parents, who were probably glad to see him leave. Go ahead and take the bed, they offered.

Then he took his most daring trip, relocating the wingless aircraft on its oversized pontoon wheels to his new home.

The Count hired a truck to pull the airplane and asked Mario Medina, Elena's sister's husband, if he would help. Mario, who had no earthly idea that he was, in the Count's mind, related to him through marriage, agreed to assist von Cosel, but knew nothing about the plane's contents.

Once they had tied the plane to the truck, they started their own little parade with the airplane as the only float. Seeing this strange airship rolling on tires large enough to fit on a tractor, slowly making its way down the streets of Key West, created a festive atmosphere. Grown-ups came out of their houses and children ran alongside while Mario, sitting on top of the cabin, waved to people sitting on their front porches.

Avoiding Duval Street, they turned right on Whitehead Street, passed the Monroe County Courthouse, and then Ernest Hemingway's house, which had one of the few swimming pools in town. Near the southernmost point of the continental United States, where Whitehead ends, they turned left on United Street.

With Elena resting comfortably, silently in her cabin, they proceeded until they reached the home of Elena's parents. Having no idea their daughter was so close to them, they waved to Mario, who waved back.

For von Cosel, the trip with his dead love was a homecoming.

It was a real triumphal ride for Elena, as in her flower decorated cabin, she reclined behind the curtained windows, victor over her grave, perhaps for good if we kept the devils away.

When the procession reached White Street, they turned right, traveling about a half a mile south until the road ended at the shore. Several hundred feet to the east of the dead-end was his new residence.

Meanwhile, in Zephyrhills in 1934, one of Carl Tanzler's two daughters suddenly died of diphtheria. The death of Crystal saddened Doris, her mother, and her surviving sister, immeasurably. Surely, their father would come home for the burial of the child he had fathered during happier times when they lived in Germany. Desperately seeking emotional and financial support, Doris wrote to her estranged husband and told him of the tragedy. After all they had been through, she needed Carl more than ever before.

Remarkably, Count von Cosel was so consumed with caring for his dead sweetheart that he ignored the emotional pleas of his lawful wife.

He didn't go to his daughter Crystal's funeral, nor did he send any money. All that he had was for his beloved Elena. He would need money to build their "castle" on the sand and to care for her.

What Carl Tanzler did to his wife in her time of need was unforgivably cruel, and the mystery of it is, Carl Tanzler wasn't the kind of person who would be intentionally mean-spirited. He had become so obsessed in his deluded make-believe world that his thoughts and sympathy were reserved for his poor dead love, whom he had sworn to restore to life, whom he had sworn to love forever more.

Photographs of his new home don't live up to his description. The type of building is similar to those on farms in south Texas—an open shed for farming equipment and an enclosed room for tools, saddles, or whatever they don't want to leave out in the open. On the left side of the picture is the shed he called a "large hangar." On the right side of the shed portion are two pieces of roofing tin he called the "folding steel doors." At the very end of the shed on the far left side of the photograph, barely visible, is the airplane. His million-volt transformer and large X-ray machine must not have taken up much of the small room he and his bride would share.

In reality, von Cosel's new home on Rest Beach was a run-down shack that had been part of the old "butcher pens" where cattle were slaughtered—the blood going directly into the sea. Not only did Mario help the Count move his airship, he helped him make the necessary repairs to the living space.

So, von Cosel embellished a bit when describing his living quarters. Nevertheless he was living in one of the most comfortable places on the island, according to Mrs. Grace Rodriguez and "G.I." Rodriguez who lived there in the 1930s.

Chapter Ten

At Rest on Rest Beach

The two years the Count and Elena spent together on Rest Beach, which he called South Beach, were the happiest of his life.

Count von Cosel was never afraid of work and there was a substantial amount to be done before the shack on the beach was transformed into a "castle." His job at the hospital was as demanding and time-consuming as always, so the construction work had to be done in his off time. This was how the indomitable Count described renovation.

> There was no house down by the beach where we could live, so I had to share the cabin with Elena to protect her against prowlers and thieves. Nothing was safe from the beachcombers at that time. There was a long concrete pier reaching into the water. On the land side, there were still a few broken cement walls standing from an abandoned factory, which I intended to use in the construction of my hangar building and laboratory for biological research and X-ray work.
>
> My first work was to level the ground. This done, I rolled the plane into the ruins. Mario Medina, who had married Elena's sister Nana, helped in doing this. Now I began to build with rocks, cement, beach sand, and sea water a square of walls, with a large opening on the lee side, large enough for the plane to get out of the building and onto the wide cement runway slip. … I did all of this work myself, in addition to attending to Elena inside the ship, as best as I possibly could.

As always, von Cosel felt that Elena was there to help and guide him.

It gave me great satisfaction to build this lab, for was it not for her sake, all of this work? Yes, I always had the feeling that she was helping me. She was indeed helping me with all of the money I had piled up around her lovely form. She knew that this was to be her castle, her birthplace for a new life, from where she would fly away with me across this wide expanse of ocean to a better world.

There was still metabolism in her body, as the chemical reactions indicated, and this would require attention. There was always a surprise awaiting me when I opened her casket; particularly so when she had been sealed up. She certainly did not like that. I was glad when, at last, the house was finished and I could leave her exposed to open air. There was no more danger of deterioration except from insects which I kept away with double screens. In an airtight metal container, the gases exhaled by the body are not carried off by diffusion but accumulate and condense into liquid form. This corrosive liquid attacks the body tissues as well as the metal container, except under proper laboratory conditions where the gases are carried away by pumping apparatus.

He all the while continued fixing up the shack.

Having laid the concrete floors, I divided the building into two sections, one side for the hangar with workshop, the other half for a laboratory, and one room where I placed my bed, a large table, the organ, and my books. In the laboratory, I installed my million-volt transformer in the middle of the floor so it would be clear of the walls and roof beams. Against the front stone wall, I placed my large X-ray machine and operating table. Along the windows on the north wall, I arranged the examination bench with microscopes, scales, etc. Along the division wall, I mounted shelves all the way up to the top for bottles, chemicals, glassware, and other supplies, with a long bench in front for analytical work. This then was the new setup where I lived all alone with my Elena. There was only one neighbor, a harmless and friendly man named Frank. Frank was an Italian fisherman who had built his own shack up against the wall of my building, as he wanted to be with me. Inside of the large hangar, I installed my electric generating plant with switchboards right against the sea wall. This supplied all of the light and power which I required; I wanted to be independent of the city electric system. The hangar could be closed up with two folding steel doors as high as the surrounding walls.

A photograph of him inside his laboratory was more consistent with his description. With a globe on the top, the million-volt transformer is a diabolical looking contraption. To von Cosel's left, padlocked, is what must be the incubator tank, and it's safe to assume Elena was inside when the photograph was taken—probably by the Count himself with the timer on his camera. On the wall, there is a fuzzy picture of what appears to be a woman. Could it possibly be Elena?

Julia Hoffman, wife of William Hoffman, the artist who painted the murals at Glenn Archer Elementary School in town, recalled an interview that she had with the doctor ... before he was found out.

"I knew Dr. von Cosel. I was going with a newspaperman from Ohio. He called me one day and said he was going out to interview Dr. von Cosel, did I want to go? I said, 'Sure.' We spent about two hours with him.

"He had a Quonset hut out here on the beach at the time. We went in, and he was building a plane to go to heaven to be with Elena. He showed us the bed she'd slept in, and how he had flowers by it and photographs and he told us how he loved her. I was looking at the plane. He said he was building a darkroom in the plane so he could develop pictures on the way to heaven. He sounded so logical, he almost had me believing him.

"I stepped up on the plane and he took my elbow and said, 'Nobody goes into that plane.'" Years later she would find out why.

His beach house may not have lived up to his fantasy, but it was still prime real estate—and a tranquil place to live. With the prevailing wind coming from the east, the Count had fewer mosquitoes to battle than those living in town, and the mosquitoes were ferocious. About the only weapon against them before insecticides was a good slap with the palm of the hand and mosquito netting.

When the north winds of winter blew forty-five miles an hour, he was on the lee side, and the sea was calm before him. Best of all, it was secluded. There were some homes on the south side of White Street, but none too close to Rest Beach. The elegant Casa Marina Hotel, built by Henry Flager to accommodate the passengers he brought down from the East on his railroad, was distant enough that few guests ventured past West Martello Towers, the abandoned, pre-Civil War brick fort located halfway between the hotel and the old butcher pens.

The Count's view was spectacular. Overlooking Hawk Channel, he could see the boats traveling east and west. When northers blew, the work boats would snuggle in, two or three hundred yards from shore, and anchor. The sun sparkling on the crystal-clear water put diamonds to shame.

Though his days of employment were numbered, he continued his duties as X-ray technician at the Marine Hospital. People still living remember vividly Count Carl von Cosel strutting assuredly to work from his new beachfront home, using his cane, not for health purposes, but in the aristocratic manner.

He had no choice but to walk because, by 1935, the end of the Great Depression was nowhere in sight. The trolleys had shut down, and the city was on the verge of bankruptcy having accumulated five million dollars in debt. With eighty percent of the population unemployed, public services like police, fire, and sanitation were almost nonexistent. Politics was no fun without any money to spend, so on July 1, 1934, the city council and the county commission turned the city over to the FERA (Federal Emergency Relief Administration).

Flager's Overseas Railroad was still running, though it was said to have been carrying nothing to nowhere.

The *Orlando Sentinel* editorialized: "Key West has been dead for fifteen years; the funeral procession had just been held up waiting for someone to pay the undertaker."

The cigar factories had moved to Tampa, and, if things weren't economically slow enough, the sponge industry coincidentally was wiped out by disease.

Surreal is the only way to describe this remote island that was becoming lost in time as each day was but another day. People went about their everyday routine completely unaffected by the rest of the world. There were chores to do, the washing and the cleaning, and meals had to be planned, yet there was a lack of urgency because there was plenty of time to get everything done. There was always tomorrow and not much reason to hurry. A few got ahead, some got behind, but most stayed about the same from day to day.

Marching briskly through this tropical lethargy was the German immigrant who took the X-rays, a Count no less: Count Carl von Cosel. Always erect, fit, and purposeful, he must have appeared sane to those who came in contact with him at his work. Who would have dreamed he had a deep, dark secret—that under the moon and the stars with the waves gently washing up on Rest Beach, he lived with a woman long dead?

In his laboratory, he began mixing solutions, testing pumps, and readying a new and improved incubator tank.

> All work [on Elena] had been for the purpose of arresting and delaying further deterioration of the body tissue. Mummification had partly set it in. This, however, is not beyond resurrection. The revival of the dried-up cells merely consumes and I never gave up hope while I have a will. Now I began mixing plasma solutions in sufficient quantities, adjusting, testing, cooling, and heating elements. I also tested the circulating pumps and electron cell, sterilizing everything, including rubber and glass connectors.
>
> And last but not least, came my sweet, patiently waiting darling herself. I placed her gently in the incubator tank on a thick layer of white felt and filled the entire tank with a clear solution of oxyquinoline sulphate of sodium at a temperature of thirty-eight centigrade, blood heat. In this solution I left her for twenty-four hours, then draining the incubator by opening the bottom valve, I refilled the tank, while the body was still wet and warm, with plasma solution of body temperature.
>
> While the tank was filling, of course, the tube of the intake was connected to the plasma tank until the incubator was filling up and overflowing through the foot valve into the filter and recharging tank. The outlet tube was then connected with the plasma vessel. The fluid was thus kept circulating automatically twenty-four hours a day at a temperature of thirty-seven centigrade.

Even though von Cosel concocted a way to circulate the liquid continuously, daily he raised her body out of the incubator and permitted her to rest a little. Then he would place her on his X-ray table for a five-minute high-voltage radiation treatment, then return her immediately into the circulating plasma bath.

Was he accurate in reporting such procedures? It is difficult to say. It's possible that the Count had electricity on Rest Beach, but, unless he was pilfering it from the hospital, the radioactive material necessary for X-rays was unavailable.

> This process I intended to keep as a routine as long as possible, checking up on temperature and reaction of the fluid every day, adding distilled water, glucose, saline, calcium, or whatever else was needed. Sometimes I had to neutralize the solution by adding hydrochloric acid.

Elena, suspended in the aquarium-like incubator tank, her weightless hair waving in a solution that was constantly in motion as the pump circulated it, was a sight that thrilled the doctor. He was sure he was beginning to make some progress toward bring her back to life.

> As weeks passed on, I noticed to my great joy and satisfaction how her form had filled out and developed. Her living contour was again restored, and she had added weight. Her limbs were filling out and her beauty became radiant, her expression showed serenity and happiness. It impressed me so much that it kept me spellbound to gaze at her over and over again in silent rapture. It had become my supreme joy to see her daily and lift the veilings to have another look at her and see how divinely beautiful she had developed. Often I kissed her rosy lips while she was lying in her bath, thereby getting always a liberal taste of the surrounding fluid myself which was indeed an analysis....
>
> Owing to some remaining defects on her left finger and right toe, caused by the burial, I wanted to continue until her total weight would reach one hundred pounds. She now weighed ninety pounds; that meant that a gain of sixty pounds had been achieved since the beginning of treatment.

To continue his quest of reviving Elena, von Cosel turned to music.

> Every evening now I sat at the organ and played to her the music she loved: Beethoven, Bach, or Wagner. It was not only my own fancy, but more than that, it was a means to apply the cosmic laws of vibration through the harmonic sound waves. These aside with electric waves, which have a positive action in a status mascendi during the formation of atomic structure. There is nothing mystical or magic about this; no, it's an exact science. Vibrations of divinely inspired harmonics differ a great deal from the vulgar kind which have destructive action.

Once again perhaps Wagner most fit von Cosel's state of mind. Wagner's divine love after death theme in *Good Friday Spell,* followed by Bach's *Toccata and Fugue in D Minor* were a fitting musical backdrop for the mad doctor.

Sadly, the beauty and peace von Cosel felt were soon to be interrupted.

> Unfortunately, I was again greatly troubled by the outside world.... Stealing and pilfering now became all too frequent. The entire area had become unsafe.... As the conditions kept getting worse, I found it necessary for Elena's safety to interrupt the incubation, temporarily at least ... so I lifted her out, dried her with alcohol and Eau de Cologne ... and dismantling the incubation assembly....
>
> She was not embalmed now after her tissues had been resurrected by the incubation period. Although her body was sterile enough, she was not safe from insects. For this reason, I thought it better to extend the silken layer protection all over the body to make sure that insects should find no exposed skin surface, and also to retard desiccation.... Oh, how marvelously beautiful she now looked with the white silk lace veils covering her down to her feet. She was so precious to me that I would take no risks. To guard her day and night, I slept right along side her at night....

As von Cosel was wholly absorbed in safeguarding Elena, he rarely took notice of anything except immediate threats to her well-being. There was a low pressure calmness preceding the big hurricane on 1935.

> Reports from Cuba and the United States weather bureaus predicted the storm center as coming in a straight line toward Key West from the southeast.... All of Key West had been preparing for the approaching storm, closing shutters, windows, and shops.... Elena had to be wrapped in her silken quilt as she was. I laid the crucifix on her breast....

Wagner would have been proud of the Count as he seated himself at the organ and began to play *Good Friday Spell*. As the winds resounded, only von Cosel's soul could hear every note over the wind and rain.

> "Elena, my darling, we are alone on this shore. The hurricane may free us both from this life, but we will cling together faithfully, you and I and our God. Death will not harm us, nor separate us any more. He who has given you to me, will not reject our souls, united as they are in His undying love...."
>
> [As the storm roared], I added Vox Celeste on the second movement. It sounded very sweet, like a chorus of angels in the high heavens, while the satanic chorus of the gale screamed against the heavenly voices of love eternal, like in a great battle.
>
> On and on I played.... It was as if heaven itself lent the strength of the forte to these harmonics of eternal love. At that moment nothing existed for me but the great sound which flowed from mine and Elena's soul united with the organ. And as the organ tones diminished in the finale, dying out faraway into the heavens with the faintest pianissimo, there was silence outside; the great battle of nature had come to an end....
>
> Then I bent down kissing Elena's coffin, embracing it, and saying:
>
> "Elena dear, God bless you. He saved Key West and all of us! Thank God."

Luckily, Key West didn't have much damage from one of the worst storms ever to hit the coast of Florida. Key Largo, Matacumbe, and Tavernier, located between Miami and Key West, took the brunt of the storm that killed many people who lived there—bodies were actually hanging from trees. The storm was so ferocious it destroyed the Overseas Railroad, cutting off the Lower Keys from the mainland. Flagler's dream-come-true had made its last run.

After the storm, people up and down the Keys began picking up broken tree limbs, opening storm shutters, and trying to figure out how best to deal with this latest, very dramatic, and bewildering event that separated Key West from the rest of the world.

For von Cosel, the only important thing that could be destroyed were his treatments of Elena and these were not greatly disturbed.

After the danger was past, I opened Elena's casket and placed her back in her bed. Now she could absorb fresh air.

Chapter Eleven
Finally, Elena Re-awakens

The Christmas which approached was to be von Cosel's best. In a photograph, Elena is lying in her bed wearing a bridal gown. To her right there is a table with a small tree decorated with holiday ornaments.

I prepared, as always, her little Christmas tree, decorating it with silver tinsel, cotton snow, and with small wax candles instead of electric bulbs. I placed the tree on a bench beside her bed with little gifts, such as picture books, chocolate, cakes, cookies, perfume, soap, face powder, etc., which she liked when alive. For me, she will never die but will live on with me, and I shall always treat and respect her as a living person.

On Christmas Eve I lit the candles on the tree, there were just thirteen of them, and placing her crucifix nearby I told her: "Elena! It is Christmas!" Then taking my seat at the organ, I played "Silent Night" until the lights on the tree were burning down. Going to her bed and seating myself beside her, I lifted her veil and kissed her on the lips:

"Elena, darling, we are all alone in this world—you and I and our God—but we are happy and contented. Let us stay together forever."

There was a small bottle of Rhine wine on the table, another Christmas gift. I opened the bottle and filled one glass, raising it with a prayer to our God for his blessing. I drank half of it and drew the other half into my mouth. Lifting her veils again, I pressed my lips firmly against hers which were open just a little. Thus slowly, I forced the wine into her mouth.... The air from my lungs entered hers and caused her

> bosom to rise. I released my lips and she breathed out again, but retained all of the wine, not a single drop spilled on her bridal array. I used this method of feeding her at different times with certain solutions when I wanted to be sure they went home where I wanted them to.

It never occurred to von Cosel to blame the deity for Elena's tuberculosis, nor was he ever angry with God's decision to take his beloved. Fatalistically, almost cheerfully, von Cosel accepted God's will and felt that what he, himself, was doing with this woman, dead for five years, was done with His blessing.

And there appeared to be signs that his ministrations were producing some good effects.

> Of course, there was no risk of infection whatever, as Elena's body was now aseptic. Her nostrils were sealed with cotton but her ears were now open. While seated close to her, I noticed what seemed like a faint breathing movement of her breast.... I got my stethoscope to listen to her chest for a while. There was no regular heart beat, but there was the sound of flowing liquid into the vessels, then a pause, then a sound of flowing again, with some kind of an irregular flutter in between.
>
> Her body was still warm to the touch since the incubation, but she had already lost considerable blood temperature. It was only natural that she was gradually cooling out again. To slow this down as much as possible, I covered her over completely with the silk quilt, at least for the duration of the cool weather.

Undressing her so she could be examined, he could hear all kinds of important sounds and apply the necessary therapy. No one else would understand, he felt. Only Elena could comprehend the importance of what was being done to her.

Unfortunately, for the Count, the peace and solitude he enjoyed at his home on the beach was interrupted in 1936 by workers from the W.P.A. (Work Projects Administration). In an effort to make the depressed national economy prosperous once again, Franklin Delano Roosevelt's New Deal instigated public works projects. The logic was, if the government put people to work on civil improvements that benefited the community, not only would the nation as a whole improve, but workers would have paychecks. Spending those paychecks on consumer goods would, in turn, jump-start the economy. Letting the despair of unemployment run its course without governmental intervention seemed too cruel. After all, wasn't the function of government to help the people?

People put to work by the New Deal included artists who were recruited to help put Key West on the map as a creative haven, an art colony (due in part to Hemingway's presence). When the W.P.A. in the Keys made the recruits wear short pants as a publicity stunt to show how good the weather was, it turned out to be one of the funniest incidents because the men working were from the mainland and had never worn shorts. Newspapers everywhere carried the story, "Workers Go To Work In Shorts."

In addition to the art projects, the W.P.A. was restoring and cleaning up the beaches, including Rest Beach. For the Count, that meant once again people were suddenly all around his private and peaceful shack. Having that many people in the vicinity made it impossible for him to use the incubator tank, and that was a shame because it was her immersions into the chemicals that had restored Elena's contour. To make matters worse, the person in charge of the beach clean-up crew had a personal grudge against the Count.

Suspending Elena's treatments in order to hide from inquisitive eyes the holy secret he guarded so patiently, the Count agonized about the welfare of his beloved.

Now von Cosel suffered another setback:

> **One morning my walls were shaken by the big explosion. The great concrete pier close to my house had been blown up by them. This made it impossible to live there any longer in safety. My house, now no longer protected from the sea, had to be abandoned. I received no compensation for this loss, nor was I provided with another house I could move into, which absolutely amounted to persecution.**

Needing another out-of-the-way place, the search for a new castle for his Elena wasn't an easy one. Finally he found, on Flagler Avenue, about two miles from "Old Town," another wooden shack meeting the most important criteria—seclusion.

> At last I found another building which was large enough, where I could move in with all my possessions. There was a scarcity of houses at the time and I was glad to take it, although it was not a suitable place for my laboratory and hangar. It took me and Frank a full month to pack up and to move my twenty truckloads of equipment, from April 30 to May 28, 1936.

Assuming that two or three of the trucks were filled with personal items, such as clothing, that still left seventeen or eighteen truckloads of inventions or junk depending on one's perspective; that didn't include the airship and the unpatented aeronautical instruments that were crammed into the cockpit. The scarcity of housing about which von Cosel complains was only a problem for him. Moving into one of the homes in "Old Town" with little or no back yard was out of the question. He obviously needed more space than the normal individual.

This was going to be Elena's fifth postmortem, post-embalmed journey and the second in his wingless airplane.

> Elena, of course, was placed comfortably in the cabin of her plane. Now with the plane hitched to my car, I taxied the airship slowly along the coast on Roosevelt Boulevard to the building on Flagler Avenue. She was the last to leave.

Roosevelt Boulevard was the indirect scenic route to his new home, and President Roosevelt was, according to von Cosel, the reason he lost his job at the Marine Hospital. In fact, in a reverse trickle-down theory, this was true. According to a former hospital employee, von Cosel didn't lose his job because he was incompetent; he was laid off, the victim of a reduced operating budget. Whatever the reason, Dr. von Cosel accepted his discharge almost graciously.

Without the interaction with his fellow workers, he soon lost almost all contact with the small community living on the other side of the mangrove trees that separated him from town.

The only regular communication von Cosel had with the townsfolk were his regular visits to the post office to pick up his monthly check, the source of which has been the subject of much speculation among those later familiar with von Cosel's bizarre saga.

One possible source was a pension for his service in the German military during World War I, a fact he may have tried to conceal by making up his life as a British subject in Australia before he was incarcerated in the Trial Bay Concentration Camp. Conceivably, in the Germany Navy, he could have been an X-ray technician who was captured at the beginning of the war and then transported to the prison in Australia for the duration. After the war, returning to Germany, he could have filled out the necessary papers to claim what he was due.

Von Cosel himself, claimed the check came from a machine shop he had owned in Germany before he immigrated to the United States. Carl explained that the shop was very successful because scientists would come to him with their ideas. It was so successful that he sold it for money down and a monthly check. However, if this were true, why then would he have immigrated to Zephyrhills intending to farm with his sister, wife, and children?

A third possible explanation came from a former co-worker who wrote a letter in von Cosel's behalf to the Government of Germany stating that the Count was impoverished. The money he received, she said, was sent from Berlin because he was a destitute German citizen living abroad. That Germany would respond with a monthly check to someone broke in Key West during a worldwide depression seems doubtful.

Another theory is that the monthly allotment could have been an inheritance. Whatever the source, it enabled the unemployed Count to live peacefully for a time, coexisting with both the supernatural and nature.

His new home was a large wood barn type structure, situated among bush and jungle scenery.

As it consisted of only two small rooms beside the shed, I made one of them my bedroom and the other a laboratory and storeroom which, however, could only hold my X-ray equipment. The organ I placed in the bedroom, also my books, a writing table and the microscopes, etc.

Frank, his fisherman friend, who had helped him load the twenty truckloads, sailed his three boats from Rest Beach to the lagoon among the mangroves where life was serene.

> Here he could go out fishing as usual, catching crawfish [Florida lobster] and plenty of other kinds; but his beloved conch shells were rather scarce in this locality. Close to the house and kitchen we planted vegetables, papayas, bananas, lime, and coconut trees; there was plenty of wood here to keep a fire going. The kitchen door, opposite the main building, was always left open as a shelter for our dogs which guarded our home.
>
> When everything was nice and clean inside the tiny bedroom and the doors and windows had been tightly screened, I opened the airplane to take out my secret treasure. I would not leave her a minute longer lonely by herself. Carrying her in my arms, I placed the coffin on my table and opened the six padlocks. After unfolding the new blue silk quilt, she came out beautiful, radiant as ever with her jewels, flowers, and bridal array. Here she could breathe fresh air again, which she needed as the air inside had an acid odor.
>
> However, there were intermittent difficulties. My power-generating machinery could not be installed at the new place; consequently, I could incubate no more until I had built a new laboratory. I decided that it was best to leave Elena exposed to the open air for a time. I knew well that it was impossible to prevent desiccation of the tissues, and that mummification would finally take place, because the small quantities of liquids I could infuse would not be sufficient to prevent it. But as long as I could prevent re-infection of the body tissues with bacteria, I was satisfied. There was nothing to prevent re-incubation later on....

Unable to incubate Elena, the most important thing he had to do was guard her from natural destruction.

> In her big bed, covered by double and triple screens all around and waterproof tent above it, she knew she was secure and she looked comfortable and contented just as if she knew.

And I am positive she did know she was lying on her own mattress on which she had died and was inviting me to her side. Now I slept by her side to be close to her and to protect her from insects and other dangers, as I could feel it for her. Whenever I discovered another leakage, I sealed it up right away with silk and wax, to stop any plasma from running away. When any part had shrunk in by loss of fluids, I filled it up with soft sterile cotton packing and overlaid it with silk and wax...

Every evening I played organ music for her and in the morning, when I had cooked my breakfast, consisting of eggs, toast, and Lipton's tea, I carried it into her room and placed it on her little table. Lifting the veil I invited her:

"Come darling, join me, our wedding breakfast."

Then, sitting down, I ate in perfect peace and contentment as I felt that she was with me and could see me. I always experienced a feeling of harmony and silent happiness as though an angel were present.

Generally at noon, Frank came back from his trip with nice fresh fish and made a fish dinner with potatoes and cabbage or macaroni....

Life once again became extraordinarily peaceful, without trauma, and then according to the Count, the miracle of miracles occurred:

On the twenty-ninth day of July, 1936, I woke up early in the morning. My eyes were wide open, I was in the full possession of my senses and faculties. No matter what people will think or say, I was ready to go out and report the news to the press that Elena had at last re-awakened to life. This reawakening was so real that I convinced myself it was not just an apparition or imagination. It was her own real body, her own personality.

As I looked at her, I noticed the fingers of her right hand moving, and taking her hand in mine, I felt how relaxed and soft it became again. Immediately thereafter, her whole arm lifted itself up and her hand pressed firmly against my face and lips as she used to do when alive, so that I could kiss it. When I kissed her hand, she opened her eyes and looked at me intently. Then, turning herself on her side toward me, she attempted to get up. I was fully awake and became alarmed, fearing that she would collapse and fall, so I spoke to her quietly:

"God bless you, Elena. I am so happy you awakened from your long sleep."

Von Cosel felt ecstasy but he also felt trepidation, not about her reawakening from the dead, but about the trauma of the move.

"I've come to stay with you for a while and keep you company," [she said].

"Elena," I answered, "... now don't be too hasty in getting up. It may exhaust your strength, my darling. Wait a little and I will make you some hot beef tea to strengthen you."

I went out at once and made hot beef tea from Liebig's Extract. When I returned in a few minutes to give her the beef tea, I found her in a state of rigidity, but still in the same position in which I had left her and looking toward me. I turned her gently back on her cushions to straighten her and gave her the hot beef tea, tasting it first myself as usual. Then I waited by her side for some time, but she remained motionless; so it transpired that this wonderfully happy awakening had ended.

Greatly upset, the Count felt he was at fault and that perhaps her second God-given chance at life had come and gone like the tide.

It gave me a lot to think of. This was metaphysical from every angle. Critically gathering and analyzing my own thoughts and movements during this phenomenon, in order to detect any possible fault on my part at this critical moment, which might have made her revert to her former state.

Was it perhaps my hesitation in the face of this unexpected phenomenon taking place? Of course, there were physical reasons, such as the absence of blood pressure.

Or was it because I left her side that her life ebbed away?

The possibility that it had all been a dream had to be ruled out by finding her in the same position.

There was little von Cosel could do without his electrical instruments to monitor the situation, so he gathered fragrant little blossoms of myrtle (more likely it was the pleasing scent of jasmine bloom) and placed them around her.

On her head he placed a wreath of flowers
Full of love he held her close to him

Eventually she, her bed, the organ, and everything smelled like this exquisite perfume, and as abruptly as Elena had reverted to her former state, she resumed communicating directly with the Count.

Insects had again begun tormenting his love, so, after a bath in chinosol and Eau de Cologne, he began to give her another layer of silk and wax. Now that she was alive, it was doubly important to pay attention to her upkeep. When he discovered he was out of silk, Elena re-awakened and, this time, it was she who came to his rescue.

"Take my bridal dress. It's soiled anyhow."

I answered: "That's a good idea, darling. I will take your bridal dress and cut out the soiled parts and there will be plenty of silk left, and I will buy you a new one tomorrow."

Now I had more than enough silk to cover her entire body for the second time and I proceeded to do so from her neck to her feet. This layer I sealed again with wax and balsam. She was doubly secure in her two silk skins. Her body was lovely and ready to be dressed up again. Once more I bought her a beautiful golden colored silk dress, trimmed with white silk lace; it matched the gold in her twenty-two carat golden crownlet and with a fragrant myrtle wreath around her auburn hair. Where was there ever such a lovely bride?

There was a distant sound immensely, eternity, millions of harmonies from this endless space striking the very foundation of our souls, it moved our souls deep down.... I realized how miserable this short life is down here, which luckily lasts but a brief spell....

The Indian Sanskrit calls it *"Devachan,"* this "Home of Souls," known more than seven thousand years. When I entered it, Elena seemed attached to my body, which, of course, is not surprising since I had promised her that wherever I went I would take her with me.

In a letter to his sister who was still living in Zephyrhills—the same small town where his other wife and his surviving forsaken child lived—von Cosel described a visit he and Elena made to heaven:

> *Key West, June 1, 1938*
> *Dear Sister:*
> *Last night I had a dream but it seemed more like reality. I spent the whole night with father and mother. Elena, too, was with me.... We were talking quietly and peacefully, when Elena, who had been in a death-like coma, woke up suddenly....*
> *It was wonderful to see her elation in this new world. She was wearing a new pink dress. The color of her eyes had changed from dark brown to blue....*
> *Now, as I write this down, I have a feeling that I have moved and am standing right on the threshold of this eternal space. It is as if only a thin veil separates me from it. I am convinced now that Mother and Father are living happily together in that eternal life, and I am so glad that it has moved so close to me or else I have moved close to it.*
> *With love, your brother Carl*

When von Cosel awoke from the dream, the only thing that consoled him was Elena's presence.

> On seeing her again at my side, I said: "All right, my darling, we will carry on the fight together until we go back. The time is short, then we will be together in the home where there is no death."
> Seeing her crucifix on the side of the bed and Saint Cecilia above, playing the organ, I sat down at the organ by the bed and played the hymn "The Home of the Soul."

Then Elena, who could now speak German, began to sing. One particular song was a favorite: '*Ach wie ist's moglich dann, dass ich Sich lassen kann,*' 'How Can I Part from Thee, How Can I Leave Thee.'

It sounded so sweet and lovely when her voice joined the organ tone.

Though her voice was as beautiful as ever, all was not well with his loving bride.

It was desiccation. She was drying out and had been losing gradually from ninety to seventy, then to sixty, then fifty, and finally down to forty pounds as I weighed her from time to time. With this loss of weight, her features would naturally change, becoming still and a little distorted when the underlying tissues fell in after dissipation of fluids, leaving empty spaces as the water evaporated.

Perhaps the Count was distracted as he pondered Elena's condition when an accident occurred. On the second of March, 1940, he slipped and fell through the deck frames of a boat on which he was working. Unable to extricate himself and having broken several ribs, he was paralyzed with pain.

My first thought was: My god, what shall become of Elena in the house if I do not return. My sweet Elena, I will join you soon.

Then I heard her voice say to me: "Take a deep breath, as deep as you can, expand your chest, then you can come home."

Broken ribs are constantly painful because they continually move as a person inhales and exhales. Only with superhuman strength was he able to crawl out of the boat and walk home. Incapacitated, agonizing and hurting, he was uncomfortable in every position until Elena instructed him to lie beside her with his back resting against her body. Only then was he able to get some sleep.

Feeling depressed—Elena was back down to forty pounds and his injury was making him feel older than his age—he began passing the time in the cemetery repairing and making new cement urns and vases to beautify Elena's mausoleum which, if all went as planned, would also be his someday.

He closed his eyes and he gently kissed her
Never again would he awaken

In the crypt, they could rest peacefully and eternally, which seemed only fitting after what they had been through together.

But dark clouds were gathering on the horizon. The ominous storm of premonition began to signal the Count that something bad was going to happen.

On three successive days, namely September 11, 12, and 13, 1940, while lying half awake, I heard Elena's voice anxiously calling me:

"Hide me, hide me somewhere." And another time: "Can't you hide me somewhere?"

Astonished at what it might mean, because, of course, I took it literally, I answered:

"Why should I hide you, Elena? You could be no safer anywhere than here in your own bed." It puzzled me also that she would not say anything more. Of course, I could have put her back into the casket, which would not have been better but worse; it would deprive her of the air which she needed.

The fourteenth of September, just before sunrise, I was awakened by Elena's body trembling all over for about a minute. I tried to soothe her trembling form with my hands and spoke to her softly:

"Elena, God bless you darling, are you going to rise? Rise if you must to our Heavenly Father. All of my love will help you on the way." When I took her hands in mine and kissed her lips, the tremor had gone.

Chapter Twelve

Nothing Stays the Same

As time passed, von Cosel continued to think his secret was safe, but his actions became suspect. He bought a lot of soap. He bought jewelry. He bought an enormous amount of Eau de Cologne. What was von Cosel doing in his shack out there on Flagler? It could have been von Cosel's friend, Frank, who began the talk, or some kids who peeked into von Cosel's home, but an ugly rumor was circulating around town.

Most people just laughed it off, but a few were taking it seriously. In Key West, where everyone eventually knows everything, it was only a matter of time before word reached Elena's sister, Nana, that her dead sister might not be resting in peace in her mausoleum.

September 28, 1940, was another of those fateful days for Count Carl von Cosel.

Nana's husband, Mario, the man who had informed the Count of Elena's death and had ridden, unknowingly, near her body when he sat atop the wingless airplane as it bumped over the red brick roads of United Street on its way to Rest Beach, again visited von Cosel's home with important news. "Elena's tomb has been broken into and the coffin tampered with."

Carl's life with Elena had been, up to this point, a very private affair. No other living souls were involved. Now, due to this latest turn of events, the drumbeat of discovery, which would ruin everything for the Count, awakened anxiety in his stomach. The voice of fear whispered to him—softly—please Lord, don't let them take her.

Accompanying Mario to the cemetery, he found Nana Medina, Elena's sister; Mr. Bethel, the cemetery sexton; and Mr. Pritchard, the undertaker.

Nana immediately insisted that the coffin be opened. With good reason, von Cosel wouldn't hear of it:

With this I flatly refused to comply.

Pritchard and Bethel, according to the Count, assured everyone that all was well in the tomb and that the inner coffin had not been opened though the outer one had. Understandably, they were not thrilled with the prospect of opening a casket that had presumably been unmolested for nine years. Undoubtedly, it would be a gruesome sight they could well do without, so they sided with the Count.

Nana was momentarily placated.

Relieved that he had, at least for the time being, been able to guard his secret, Carl returned to his home way out on Flagler Avenue, separated from those who wouldn't understand, and told Elena of her sister's behavior. He talked to her and caressed her that evening while the sweet smell of rain, and the distant rumblings of thunder permeated the night.

It was a moment of serenity not to last. On October 1st, Mario returned and summoned von Cosel to the cemetery again, only this time there was a crowed when Nana confronted Carl and emotionally demanded the coffin be opened. Through the Count's eyes, Nana was a selfish spiteful serpent who would not allow love to triumph. Through less biased eyes, Nana, who was ill and would also die from tuberculosis, was concerned about the eternal peace of her dear sister.

Carl chided her:

> "You ought to be ashamed of yourself, talking like that at the grave of Elena. She is an angel, but not you. I can clearly see that you don't love her, nor are you interested in her safety. All you seem to be interested in is to strip your sister again of her jewels; that's why you broke into the tomb."
>
> The sexton had handed me a piece of rusty iron, bent from the strain of wrenching the locks from the cement walls, and a pair of old rusty scissors, used apparently to dig the window panes out of the door. These I turned over to the sheriff for fingerprints. (No fingerprints were taken, however).

Ironically, von Cosel was accusing Nana of attempting to rob the grave that he knew was empty because he had already removed the contents.

After a while Nana spoke again, but this time plaintively:

"Please open the tomb and let me see Elena inside her coffin or I believe I will go crazy. If only I could see her to know that she is all right, I'll be satisfied."

Well, this sounded sensible and fearing that she might become hysterical and since she was the only sister remaining, I decided to convince her and let her see that Elena was perfectly safe. So I said to her: "All right, Nana, I don't want you to go crazy, I will let you see Elena. Let's talk this over in peace and arrange it between ourselves. This is not a public affair."

"Where do you want us to go?" she asked.

"Well, to your house, which is nearest from here," I answered.

"No," she replied. "Not in my place."

The Count was not able to comprehend that finding Elena was exactly what Nana was afraid of. She didn't want this eccentric German whoever-he-was in possession of her sister Elena's dead body. The thought of it was so repulsive, she had to make sure it wasn't true—or, heaven forbid, find out if it was.

"Well, then, let's drive down to my house."

She agreed and so we drove straight for my house on Flagler Avenue.

At my home she invited another woman who was in the car to come in, which, however, I vetoed as she did not belong to the family.

When coming inside my rooms, Nana stayed back near the door, while her young husband Mario came along with me to see where Elena's bed stood. He exclaimed:

"Here is Elena's bed, Nana."

I invited Nana:

"Come here, Nana, and see how beautiful Elena is resting in her bed in her silken garments and with all her jewelry. Come and see, she could not have it better anywhere. I think that will pacify you now."

As Nana came alongside the bed, the Count lifted the curtain and there she was, his Elena.

In the dark, candlelit room, at first Nana couldn't believe her eyes and refused to accept that this patchwork body, reconstructed with wax and cosmetics was her sister. Turning to the Count, she asked how long the body had been there, and he replied, seven years.

> Nana gripped her husband's arm and said:
> "Let's get out of here, I feel bad. Let's go back to the cemetery and open the vault to see what's inside the coffin."

According to von Cosel, her husband answered:

> "What's the use now, you have seen that she is here."
> But she persisted in pretending that it was not Elena and Mario shrugged:
> "I don't know what to do with Nana, she's crazy."
> "I think so too, but you ought to teach her some common sense," I said. "I am not going to open the vault and coffin. Not after showing Elena to her."

It was an eerie encounter that both frightened and horrified Nana. Later, Nana and Mario's recollection of the encounter differed considerably from the version von Cosel described so calmly and rationally. When they told their version of what had transpired, it was not Nana whom Mario called crazy.

> They both went to the car, but before going away, Nana called me:
> "I want you to put Elena back into the vault, but I want to be present to see that she lies in the coffin, do you hear?"
> "Elena and I will go back to the vault together when our time is up, but not right now. I don't see why you should worry about her now. You never looked after her for the past nine years. She has been under my care all these years. I have paid all of her expenses, not you; you forget that I own that tomb with everything that is inside, not you!"

Though von Cosel couldn't comprehend Nana's reaction, it should have dawned on him that Nana and Mario's discovery would not end there.

In the shack, the lonely German immigrant sat down beside his lovely Elena and tried to soothe her with reassuring words.

> "She cannot injure us, no matter what comes, don't worry, darling. And as Nana is only after your jewels, let me take care of them for you until the trouble is past, then you will get them all back, sweetheart."
> She released them easily and I locked them safely away in a little casket.

And for the next five days he sat alone with his dead love, wondering what was going to happen—hoping they would be able to stay together.

Not only for Carl (Tanzler) von Cosel, but for the world, these were days of trepidation and torment.

On October 4, the headlines in the *Key West Citizen* were:

DETROIT [TIGERS] COLLECTED 13 HITS
TO CAPTURE 3RD GAME OF SERIES

and

AXIS POWERS PREPARE FOR NEW ATTACKS

A whistling bomb exploded (at a location in London, England, not revealed for security reasons) almost killing King George.

October 5, 1940, the headlines read:

EXPECT JAPAN TO JOIN AXIS POWERS

That very same day, a motorcade, headed by two sheriffs, then the justice of the peace, followed by the funeral car and several other cars stopped in front of von Cosel's house. As he opened the screen door, the sheriff presented von Cosel with a warrant charging him with being in possession of a dead body.

> Politely he asked me whether I was the person whose name was on the paper. I answered yes, this was my name. He then asked me to show him the body. After seeing the body in bed, he inquired if it was true that I had this body in my possession for over seven years. I answered in the affir-

mative.

"And who is she?" [asked the sheriff]

"She is my bride, Elena Hoyos."

He asked further whether I had a certificate for the body.

"Yes, I have."

"Show it to me, please."

After getting out her certificate from Elena's records, I showed it to him. He shook his head:

"This is her certificate of death; that isn't the certificate we want."

"I do not know of any other certificate required for the dead."

"I am sorry, we have to take you to the courthouse, as you have no certificate. You may explain in court."

So I followed the sheriff into the car. I noticed the funeral car driving up and two attendants stepping in my door. They carried Elena out in a wicker basket, putting her in the car. This audacity enraged me. I made a move to stop them. The sheriff held me on each side, pacifying me, telling me everything was all right, but I said:

"There is no security for my house, when strangers are going in and out at liberty. I protest against this violation of my rights."

The sheriff answered:

"We are having the body placed in the funeral home where it is safer until your case is settled. Then you may get it back. I will see that nothing is removed and lock the doors and bring you the keys."

For the last time, von Cosel looked over his shoulder at Elena. He caught a glimpse of her face as the men solemnly slid the wicker body casket into the back of the black hearse.

After bringing me the keys, the car started toward town, where I was taken to the courthouse.

Now there began cross examination by the sheriff. All about my past experience with Elena, her death, burial and disinterment, reinterment in the tomb, etc., etc. Finally, he dug out the great old U.S. Law Statute book, showing me the paragraph under which I had been indicted.

Of course, there was no way the Count could have foreseen how much trouble and how much publicity his daring love affair was going to generate, and this is where the heart aches for Carl von Cosel as he stubbornly clung to his illusions.

For better or for worse, von Cosel's life changed dramatically the moment he was arrested. Literally, overnight, he went from a solitary eccentric in a remote island town to an internationally known figure. From obscurity to fame, instantaneously, Count von Cosel became a celebrity.

As he arrived at the courthouse, flashbulbs from reporters' cameras exploded. Word had been circulating around the courthouse that someone was about to be arrested for sleeping with a corpse. The news spread like wild fire through southern Florida—reporters and photographers in a feeding frenzy were already there and more were on their way to Key West.

> The sheriff was a kindhearted man; I saw how his eyes filled with tears as he said:
>
> "I see there is a wrong being done to you, you are not guilty in the sense of the charges in the book. You did build the tomb and made it beautiful at your own expense. I am sorry, but we have to keep you here until the case is cleared in court."
>
> By this time the place was crowded with photographers, taking shots from right and left. It annoyed me and I asked the sheriff, why all this publicity. He answered smiling:
>
> "They are photographers of the press."
>
> "Why do you permit this nuisance?"
>
> "Well, it is custom, our liberal government gives freedom to the press."
>
> Then came the order by Justice of Peace, Esquinaldo, that I be held on $1,000 bail until the court's disposal of the case.
>
> I was taken to the county jail for retention. But first, I handed the sheriff Elena's jewel case to lock up in the office safe. I had picked it up at home before leaving.

Astounded and bewildered by all the attention, von Cosel was booked at the county jail on the charge of "wanton and maliciously demolishing, disfiguring, and destroying a grave."

Feeling deserted and alone for the first time since Elena had come to live with him, he said:

> This night in jail was hard for me. When I laid down on the cot, staring at the barred window, I finally prayed: If this be my final end, then, God unite me with my Elena forever, as a spiteful world makes our peaceful existence impossible.

To his mind, it was as if his prayer was heard:

> A band began playing somewhere in the neighborhood. It was a cradle song, over and over again, to lull me to sleep. Suddenly, Elena's spirit was standing before me in her bridal dress, bending down, embracing, and kissing me:
> "Suffer it for me, it won't be long, then you will be free." Then it was dark again. As she had become invisible, I turned over with my face against the wall, as I did not want to see the bars. I slept peacefully until morning.

In the lead paper, although he didn't read it, von Cosel was highlighted: October 7, the *Key West Citizen:*

HOLD VON COSEL ON MALICIOUS AND WANTON CHARGES
WARRANT SERVED THIS AFTERNOON; CASE ATTRACTS INTEREST THROUGHOUT NATION

At a late hour this afternoon, county officials were investigating the process of law to follow in the case of Carl Van Cosel, who has been formally charged with malicious and wanton disfigurement of a burial vault in the city cemetery when he removed the body of Elaine Hoyo Mesa to his home in defiance of state health laws.

Key West was abuzz with talk today concerning one of the most interesting stories ever to break in this or any other city of the nation, and, according to observance, the rest of the nation is going to hear of the story too, for two leading news services have placed it on their wire and telephoto releases to subscribing members.

Carl Tanzler Van Cosel, a resident of Key West for the past ten years is the center of attention here today, following the revelation yesterday that he had kept the body of his sweetheart, Elena Hoyos Mesa, beside him in a room of his isolated house on Flagler Avenue for the past seven years.

According to the scientist, he had come to the end of a long trail which started with a dream he had back in Germany which had compelled him to search the world over for the "beautiful lady" pictured in that vision. He found her in Key West, only to lose her, at least temporarily, when she died at the hospital and was buried in the city cemetery.

Then followed the train of events, just now uncovered, which at once lifts Van Cosel to a position of national interest and, except for the gruesome aspects of the case, to recognition as one of the truest of romanticists of all time.

Little did the county and city authorities think, about two weeks ago when investigating reports of "grave robbing" in the city cemetery, that those investigations would be followed by the astounding news....

For it was from one of those vaults that the body of Elaine had been removed—but not recently. Over seven years ago the crime, as some call it, was committed. Placed in a vault built by himself with parental permission, the beautiful young lady was visited regularly by her aged lover, and the story now released is that he could not bear to think of her body slowly rotting away to "nothingness," and it was then, approximately two years after her death, that he was determined to take her remains and do what he could to preserve them.

In brief, these facts stand out in the arrest made yesterday, following discovery of the body on a bed next to one on which Van Cosel slept.

The search warrant was sworn out by relatives of the dead girl, who had been suspicious for some time that she was not within the vault. Deputy sheriffs Bernard Waite and Ray Elwood made the arrest and placed Van Cosel in jail to await a hearing late this afternoon.

The body had been excellently modeled out of wax, presumably, bit by bit, as flesh decayed. Relatives declared she looked "surprisingly like she did in life." It was covered with mosquito netting to keep insects away....

How he made the removals is a mystery to Key Westers today. The first move, from the vault to this home, appeared to have been the most difficult. In the second instance, authorities believed that he employed an old airplane he had purchased trailing it behind an auto hired for the purpose, the owners of which little suspected the strange cargo they were hauling.

Of scientific turn of mind and showing evidence of high training in chemistry, it is thought that Van Cosel had invented special processes to defeat effects of decomposition, especially in regards to odors that otherwise would have been noticed near his home.

In jail, waking up to unfamiliar surroundings, the Count had no idea that he was already a newspaper headline. Feeling bewildered, alone, having lived a solitary existence with Elena these seven years, he was doubly surprised when visitors came to the jail offering help and support.

> As soon as I woke up, a friend came. Looking through the iron barred window, he comforted me, offering me help. Shortly after breakfast, more friends arrived, offering help, asking me if they could bring some fruits and milk, and informing me that Frank would stay on my premises on guard day and night until my return. They promised to bring food for him as well as for the thirteen dogs. Now this was quite a substantial help to me. I had not known I had such good friends.

In the afternoon, a lady brought fruits and sweets and she too promised that von Cosel's home and his dogs would be taken care of. Nor were they the only consolers:

> And in the evening, I was surprised by the good Samaritan, Señorita Marguerita, a young Spanish friend who knew Elena well. She consoled me kindly, bringing cookies, fruits,

sweets, and hot tea for my supper. With my Elena taken from me, I had felt utterly lost; now I learned there were good people left in this world.

Then the mysterious band again serenaded the Count on his second night of incarceration. The next day brought some good fortune. First, the sheriff introduced him to attorney Louis Harris who offered to defend him in court without charge if von Cosel would give him the authority, which he gladly did.

HARRIS VOLUNTEERS DEFENSE
SERVICES TO DR. VON COSEL

Louis A. Harris' entry into the Dr. von Cosel case as volunteer defense attorney, representing the scientist at the hearing held and now preparing defense arguments for the trial to be held next month, has caused considerable favorable comment on the part of Key West's residents.

"Of course," Mr. Harris stated to the *Citizen* today, "it was a natural thing for me to do." This by way of disclaiming credit for the gesture. "I've been volunteering my services, just as I am in this unusual case, for many, many years—even as any honest lawyer would do.

It was recalled today that Mr. Harris, as Key West's oldest and most experienced attorney, has had a varied career in practicing his profession....

Raised in Key West, he graduated from the old Sears School here and then entered Tulane University....

Specializing in Criminal Law, it has been stated that Mr. Harris is one of the ablest lawyers in the branch of law in all of Florida.

One of the amazing things was the way people reacted to von Cosel's arrest. Public sympathy for him was immediate. Interestingly, women and men showed different emotions. Women thought that what the Count had done was marvelously romantic. Men, on the other hand, while sympathetic, were not nearly as sentimental as the women.

At noon, the jailer told the Count that a crowd of young ladies had come all the way from Tampa. Because there were too many to let inside, he allowed the Count to greet his admirers out in the front yard:

> I went outside to the young ladies, all pretty girls, who shouted: "We have all come from Tampa to see you. We are cigar makers from the Tampa factory, and we have read all about you in the papers. We wish you luck and that you will win out and get your Elena back."
> "We are all for you," said one pretty speaker in a beautiful black silk dress.
> They were such a delightfully happy lot....

They all shook hands and the girls offered him money they had collected, which the Count tried to refuse, until he realized that they would be offended if he didn't accept their generosity.

> They finally took leave with kind and sincere wishes. How nice and sweet it was of these young girls, who were motivated by true benevolence. God will be with them all and bless them.

Later in the afternoon, Father Moreaux, the priest who baptized Elena, came by. Von Cosel said:

> He offered his help, but I did not see any need for help for myself.

Von Cosel's thoughts, as they had been from the moment they'd met, were only on Elena, who now he felt had no one to care for her.

> "I am all right. The one who needs help and protection and who cannot defend herself is Elena, since she has been taken away from me."
> He said he thought she was safe enough while in the custody of the undertaker where she is now, but I had my doubts. And later it proved that I was right.

Chapter Thirteen

Order in the Court!

The media frenzy heightened as the bizarre events transpiring proved to be just as mesmerizing to the public as to the principals involved.

On October 7th, the *Miami Herald,* then in its twenty-ninth year of publication, front page screamed a large bold headline:

**DEAD GIRL'S HIGHLY EDUCATED
LOVER SEES NO WRONG IN REMOVING
HER FROM CRYPT**
HOLDER OF NINE UNIVERSITY DEGREES SITS IN
JAIL DAZED BY EVENTS; TELLS OF TRYING TO
RESTORE LIFE
by Earl Adams
Herald Staff Writer

Key West, Fla., Oct. 7—A man with nine college degrees, whose fantastic love affair has startled this island city, sits in a jail cell here bewildered and puzzled as to how he committed a crime removing from the crypt the remains of the pretty young woman he idolized in order to bring her back to life.

Carl Tanzler von Cosel, native of Dresden, Saxony, Germany, today told police he believed he could restore life to Elena Milagro Hoyos, twenty-two-year-old matron who died nine years ago. He related how he slept beside her carefully preserved body for seven years and how he experimented with all his medical skill to bring back the woman with whom he was madly in love.

He was arrested Sunday at his home, part of a dirty, ramshackle warehouse, where the lifelike body of the young woman lay in bed and charged with removing a body from its grave without permission.

Monday the body was removed to a funeral home where hundreds of Key West residents crowded in to view the young woman reconstructed and preserved in wax. Morticians said that even the eyes are artificial.

MET HER IN THE HOSPITAL

Von Cosel met and fell in love with the young girl while she was being treated for tuberculosis at a hospital where he was employed....

Driven by hopeless love, he even connected a telephone to the vault from his home so "I could talk with her on rainy days."

"The wooden coffin was placed inside a galvanized container and the container inside of a steel coffin," von Cosel said.

"About three weeks after she had been placed in the vault, I opened the steel casket and then a small hole in the galvanized container, and there was an awful odor. I then opened the wooden coffin and there were many vermin there. I decided then and there that I would take the remains and preserve them for me always."

KEEPING HIS PROMISE

"I promised Elena before she died that I would take care of her always...."

Key West was the perfect stage for this unfolding drama with its exotic but laid back atmosphere, where Hemingway strode and other characters walked the streets. The hearing was scheduled for late in the afternoon allowing people to take care of the pesky, day-to-day business before the curtain went up.

Meanwhile, the press reported on the backstage goings-on breathlessly.

On October 8th, the *Key West Citizen* headline read:

VAN COSEL TO FACE HEARING TODAY AT FIVE O'CLOCK
ENRIQUE ESQUINALDO, JR., WILL PRESIDE AT SESSION AT COURTHOUSE; SCIENTIST UNRUFFLED

Carl Tanzler von Cosel will be questioned this afternoon at five o'clock at a hearing at the county courthouse presided over by Peace Justice Enrique Esquinaldo, Jr., with all court attaches present, including the two arresting officers, deputies Bernard J. Waite and Ray Elwood.

Upon the findings at this hearing will rest the sculptor-scientist's chances of obtaining freedom from charges filed by the county, or whether he will have to stand trial in criminal court for violation of a state statute prohibiting disturbance of any kind to graves or vaults and removal of dead bodies without proper permit.

All day long yesterday and continuing this morning, hundreds of Key Westers and visitors called at the Lopez Funeral Home to view one of the strangest sights ever beheld—the remains of the long-dead Elena Hoyos Mesa, past all recognition as a human body, modeled, by the skillful hands of von Cosel, into a wax-like statuette.

Sympathy on all sides were expressed today for the scientist, and the general hope advanced was that the state would see fit to free him.... It is admitted, though, that no longer should he be allowed to keep the remains of his dead sweetheart, and this, it was understood, is just what the relatives of the dead girl will insist on.

Legally, there were three aspects von Cosel had to deal with. First, there was the original charge: "wantonly and maliciously demolishing, disfiguring, and destroying a grave."

The second legal problem was von Cosel's sanity. A three-man panel of doctors was assembled to make the determination.

The third legal hurdle the Count faced involved another law under which von Cosel could be prosecuted. As Judge Lord authoritatively pointed out to von Cosel after the hearing: "The unauthorized disinterring of the body of a deceased human being is an indictable offense, both at common law and by statute, regardless of the motive, or purpose."

Von Cosel appeared to be holding up under the ordeal. One of the jail deputies reported he was eating well and seemed willing and reconciled to cooperating with the officials.

At this point, journalists from around the world, fatigued by con-

stant tidings of war, caught wind of the incredible story and began
streaming into Key West. They joined the local citizens whose mun-
dane, everyday life was now punctuated by excitement.

People began gathering on the front lawn of the courthouse several hours before the hearing. Though it was cooling down as the
shadows grew longer, the weather was the last thing on people's
minds as the hour approached. When the doors were opened, there
was a log jam at the entrance as everyone, including the out-of-town
reporters, raced for the few available seats in the courtroom. The
ensuing confusion and the whispering when those admitted saw the
principals delayed the proceedings briefly.

Somberly, Mrs. Mario Medina, Elena's sister, stood off to one
side of the courtroom, wearing a light-print summer dress.

The tragic star ... Count Carl von Cosel, was seated beside his attorney at a long polished table in the center of the room.

The dual-paneled, sash windows were open, and the Hunter ceiling fans were moving the air enough so that Louis Harris, who was
donating his legal expertise to defend the Count, was almost comfortable in a light-weight suit and tie.

Large glass ashtrays were strategically located, and as always, the
cigarette smoke irritated the Count who had never liked tobacco.
Looking forward and saying nothing, he sat erectly, his bow tie tied
perfectly under his imperial beard. The round, gold-framed glasses
catching the light were a fitting touch for a brilliant scientist. He
bore himself as though he were about to attend an official state
function honoring the Czar of Russia, not a courtroom hearing.
However, his attire drew gasps. The black shiny lapels of his tuxedo
jacket glistened under the seventy-five-watt illumination glowing
from the frosted glass globe lamps on the fans whose blades slowly
whirled below the varnished tongue and groove wood ceiling. And
when he stood, it could be seen that he wore tennis shoes on his
feet.

A hush enveloped the room when, at 5:30 p.m., the bailiff announced the Honorable Peace Justice Enrique Esquinaldo:

"October 8, 1940. Good evening, ladies and gentlemen, officers
of the court. (deliberate pause) The purpose of this hearing is to determine whether a Mr. Carl von Cosel....

"Count Carl von Cosel, Your Honor. My name is Count Carl von
Cosel."

"Count Carl von Cosel," conceded the judge who realized from the outset this was not going to be an easy or routine evening. "The purpose of this hearing is to gather information. Based on this information, the Florida State Attorney who represents the State of Florida will, at a future date, determine whether Count Carl von Cosel, has, in fact, broken any laws. This, I would like to emphasize, is a hearing. It is not a trial. Guilt or innocence will not be determined here today. If, as a result of this hearing, charges are forthcoming, and, you, Count von Cosel, are tried and convicted at a criminal proceeding, you will be liable for up to $500 in fines and up to two years in jail.

"The first witness today is Mrs. Florinda Medina. Mrs. Medina, state your name and your relationship to the deceased."

Elena's sister, known as Nana, walked slowly to the witness box. Her nervousness was visible.

"My name is Florinda Milagro Hoyos Medina, and I am the deceased's older sister," she replied as she shifted her matronly body in the polished, hard-backed courtroom chair. She felt put on the spot even though she had done nothing wrong; nor had she done anything she regretted.

"Would you tell the court what you found when you went with Count von Cosel to his home?"

"I became suspicious that something ... peculiar was going on when Count von Cosel quit visiting the crypt he built for Elena. From time to time, people, friends of mine, told me of the rumors that were going around town. I thought little of it, yet they kept insisting that Elena might not be where she was supposed to be. Looking back, I suppose I should have acted on these suspicions sooner. I suppose I should have known something was terribly wrong, but I couldn't imagine someone taking my sister's body from the tomb. Who could imagine someone keeping a corpse in their home for seven years? The time finally came when I could no longer ignore the whispers. I had no choice but to confront von Cosel.

"Without hesitating, he told me that she was in his home. He took me there and then excitedly asked me in to see how 'beautiful' she was in her silken garments and jewelry. He kept insisting she was safe there."

Justice Esquinaldo had to quiet the uproar from the overflowing courtroom with his gavel. "Ladies and gentleman, please. Mrs.

Medina, would you describe what you saw?"

"Your Honor, it was the most grotesque thing I have even seen in my life. Her hair was still on her head. She had glass eyes. Her arms and legs were like sticks with stockings. It was a monster. It was horrible. What I saw will haunt me for the rest of my life."

"What did you do then?"

"What could I do? I tried to be reasonable. I asked him to return her body to her casket and place the casket back in the crypt where it belonged. I told him I wouldn't say a word to anyone if he would do that. It was the only sane thing to do. When he refused, I contacted the sheriff who arrested him. The funeral home took her body to the mortuary, and we all know what has happened since."

"You say Count von Cosel refused to return the body to the crypt?"

"If he had just taken her back," Nana fought to control her emotions. "Oh, if only he had taken her back where she belonged," she replied bitterly as she turned to the people in the courtroom. "I hear you snickering. I've heard the laughter behind my back. You think this terrible, terrible thing Count Carl von Cosel has done to my poor sister is some kind of joke. Well, you are every bit as sick as this mad man." She pointed directly at von Cosel and stared him in the eye.

"Your Honor, I can explain," calmly responded the Count.

"I'm sure you can!" exclaimed Nana. "Just like you explained to the reporters who were hanging around you like you were some kind of hero. How would they feel if their dead sister was in the hands of a demented doctor?"

She turned and locked eyes with the justice. "Something else I'd like to know. Why won't the doctors who examined Elena's body make their findings public? What has von Cosel done to my sister's body? Was he doing something too horrible for words?"

Justice Esquinaldo was forced to ask the question he had hoped to avoid, "Count von Cosel, did you at any time during the more than seven years you had her ... kept her, whatever.... Did you at any time sexually molest the body of Elena Hoyos?"

Defiantly, he replied, "No, Your Honor, I did not." In a lower voice he elaborated, "She was mummified."

Adamantly, Nana countered, "Your Honor, I want my sister buried somewhere that this so-called Count can't find her. I hope, from the bottom of my heart, that von Cosel will be charged and punished for this outrageous crime."

"I understand, Mrs. Medina, and I thank you for your cooperation. You may step down."

He called Count von Cosel to the stand. "Count von Cosel, state your name and occupation."

"My name is Count Carl von Cosel and I am a chemist, engineer, physicist, scientist, roentgenologist with degrees in philosophy, psychology, and medicine."

"Count von Cosel, how did you become acquainted with Elena Hoyos?"

"She was my patient and later became my bride. She has been my wife since she accepted my ring. I fell in love with her the first time I saw her. She was the woman I had been searching for all of my life."

The crowded courtroom was silent except for an occasional cough and the rustle of clothing. The gallery had been waiting to hear what von Cosel had to say and was mesmerized by the way he openly and sincerely described what he had done for love. To some, what he was saying was so ludicrous it was almost laughable, but to others, it wasn't.

"I painted pictures of her even before I met her for the first time in the old Cosel manor in Germany, then again in Italy. I kept searching. It was a divine odyssey that took me to Australia where she again sat beside me while I played my organ."

Attorney Harris interrupted von Cosel, "And then you came to Key West and found that lady, the spirit of your dreams, and lost her again, didn't you?"

Von Cosel spoke with a quiver in his voice. "Yes, sir, she is still with me right here and now in this hall. I told her no matter what happened to her, I would take care of her in life and in death. She was my bride when she accepted my proposal of marriage and I regard her as my wife. Her death sealed our bond."

"Did you take the deceased from her crypt, Count von Cosel?" asked the justice with a hint of sympathy in his otherwise judicious voice.

"I built the monument with my own two hands. I've watched over her for all of these years. I didn't want anything to harm her. She was safe with me."

Several women in the courtroom were audibly weeping.

"How long ago was it you took the body out of the crypt to your house?"

"It was months after she was placed in the tomb, pretty close to eight years ago."

"What exactly did you find when you disinterred her? What did she look like?"

"It was disturbing. Everything was a mess. Obviously, the morticians hadn't followed my instructions. The odor that resulted from their failure to embalm the casket was quite strong."

The quiet tension of the courtroom was broken. What he had seen was something everyone in their thoughts and whispers had pondered; not only their thoughts of the young dead woman but many had wondered about the effects of their own death and now knowing the details of what Elena had looked like was disquieting.

"Order! Order!"

Attorney Harris brought silence back to the courtroom when he asked, "Did you have the idea that her spirit would unite with her body and commune with you?"

"I resurrected her. I brought her back to life, Your Honor."

"How did you remove Elena's bones from the crypt to your house?"

"I removed the casket from the crypt into a car outside of the cemetery and drove alongside the airplane, placing it in the cabin."

"Did you meet anybody during this work, did anybody help you and if so, who was the person, as the casket must have been heavy?"

"No, sir, I did not meet a living person during my work, except the driver of the car outside, who helped me to lift the casket up into the plane, that was all, and I don't know his name."

"Didn't the taxi driver ask you what it contained?"

"No. He asked no questions, I paid for the service."

"Did you not move the airplane to the beach afterward?"

"Yes, I did. Mario Medina did the moving!"

"Medina, is that true, did you do the moving?"

"Yes, sir, I moved the airplane to the beach, but I didn't know that Elena was inside."

Harris brought silence to the loud whispers in the courtroom when he asked again,

"Did you have the idea that her spirit gave you advice?"

"Yes, so it did. Many times her spirit gave me advice even about the organ, also technical advice. Whenever I do not know what to do, she tells me. She also told that this trouble was coming and asked me several times to hide her body. 'Elena,' I asked, 'why should I hide you?' but she said no more and a week later the trouble came."

"How would it affect you if that body were taken from you?"

"I would feel lost. I had promised her I would keep and protect her against destruction for the rest of my life, even at the sacrifice of my own life. It may endanger my own life."

"How long do you think her body will last in the condition it is now?"

"Indefinitely."

"Do you think there is still life in the body which could be resurrected?"

Von Cosel's voice was passionate. "There is always life left in the body which can be resurrected by special methods, such as incubation. It's not the physical body. The physical body is asleep. The eyes are in darkness, but the ears can still hear. That's why I placed Elena close to the organ so she could hear the music, heavenly music. I put the pipe organ right beside her bed. Every night I played for her.... Daily I fed her my formula. She needs my powerful X-ray machine to stimulate cavities in her body...."

The Judge interjected over the objection of Attorney Harris:

"Sir, you have had her body in your possession for seven years, seven years, and she appears to be completely dead, lifeless, not alive. It seems to me that you don't understand. Count von Cosel, listen to me very carefully. What is left of Elena Hoyos is going to be buried. As the presiding justice of this hearing, that is my decision. The State Attorney will decide whether or not to bring you to trial."

The room was pin-drop quiet. Von Cosel broke the silence.

"Now may I have Elena's body back?" von Cosel demanded.

"No! No, you may not! You may not have her body back. She is going to be buried. Mrs. Medina is her only living relative, and she wants her buried. You are no relative to Mrs. Hoyos. You have no claim to the body."

In a rage, von Cosel exclaimed, "You can't do this to me! This isn't justice. Her father gave her to me. I paid for everything, everything, the funeral, the caskets, the mausoleum. She is mine. To take her from me will mean the end of everything. You are forcing me to break my sacred promise to Elena.

Nana Medina could no longer restrain herself. "Von Cosel—Elena is going to be buried in the ground and rot like all of her ancestors!!"

"Order! Order in the court!" The gavel pounded and the judge paused for the courtroom to quiet.

"Mrs. Medina, I understand and sympathize with you. Never have I encountered anything like this. You have my sympathy for what you have gone through and the carnival atmosphere surrounding this bizarre affair. Regardless of the Count's guilt or innocence, this court will honor your request to have the body of Elena Hoyos buried. Because of the circumstances surrounding this case, only relatives will be told where the grave is. Count von Cosel, I am ordering you to return to this courtroom, Thursday, October 10, 1940, for psychiatric evaluation. You will be held under $1,000 bail until I have made my decision. This hearing is adjourned."

Running to phone in their stories, reporters narrowly missed colliding with the townspeople. The newspapers had a banner morning. The first story to surface read:

PROTESTS LOVE OF CORPSE IN 3-HOUR HEARING, JAILED
By Jeanne Bellamy
Herald Staff Writer

KEY WEST, Fla., Oct 8.—This tawdry doll is the dream of a lifetime. To this graybeard, she is immortal beauty of body and spirit. They'll never shake him out of that dream.

They led him to a chair on a platform Tuesday and asked him matter-of-fact questions about her, but his low voice, almost a whisper, put a spell on the 200 pairs of staring eyes and ears strained to catch his words: "I know she is always with me. She is right here with me in this hall."

He wasn't talking about the bones of Elena Hoyos Mesa, dead nine years. Covered with wax and white paste, they were lying half a mile away in a frame building, a sideshow for some 5,000 men, women, and children who trooped past to gape at the tiny effigy.

"I can do better," he told the circle of faces in the courtroom.

They kept pressing forward, standing on chairs and tables, to hear the frail man who fingered his wavy beard and looked at his questioners through metal-trimmed spectacles that had slipped down slighting on his nose.

Electric lights had replaced the orange gleam of sunset in the big square courtroom before they let him leave at the end of the three-hour hearing. He walked out erect in his black wool suit with old-fashioned satin lapels on coat and vest. His sockless feet in white tennis shoes moved softly back toward the jail cell where he was to stay for lack of $1,000....

"That has become a sacred promise, a holy conviction, in my mind and body.

"She was my wife. She accepted my proposal of marriage.

"I built her monument with my own hands and watched over her so that nothing would happen to her. I think I have done my best...."

He said that he hired a taxicab to take him to the cemetery at dusk. Von Cosel himself removed the sealed, galvanized container from the coffin, placed it in the car, and had the driver help him lift it into the airplane he kept near the Marine Hospital. He said he did not know the driver's name, and the man knew nothing about the nature of the errand.

GAVE ULTIMATUM

Mrs. Medina said she gave von Cosel an ultimatum—he must place Elena's remains in the mausoleum within a week or she would proceed against him. At the end of the week, she obtained the warrant which brought his arrest last Sunday.

Medina and a friend of the couple, Miss Celinda Medina, who went with them to von Cosel's house but did not go in, corroborated this testimony.

Mrs. William Sawyer, custodian of the cemetery, told of finding the glass door on the front of the vault broken and reporting this fact to Mrs. Medina, the step that prompted her to question von Cosel.

Otto Bethel, sexton at the cemetery, verified dates in the case.

Reginald Pritchard, operator of the funeral home employed by von Cosel to conduct Elena's funeral and later disinter the body for replacement in the mausoleum, was the only defense witness in addition to the prisoner. Pritchard said Elena's father, before he died, signed an authorization for the disinterment to be performed under von Cosel's supervision and at his expense.

LIKE A WAX FIGURE

Asked how the remains looked today, Pritchard said, "If I went to see a wax figure, I would see the same thing."

The effigy, dressed in a blue rayon robe is the biggest sightseeing attraction in Key West at the moment. All day, carloads of people drive up, augmented by others on bicycle and on foot, to walk past the tiny figure. A square of cheesecloth covers the chalky face with its glass eyes and matted wig of short, straight, dark brown hair.

The shoulders and hip bones protrude sharply under the robe. The arms and legs are like sticks, and the gaunt hands lie stiffly at each side. A pair of black house slippers, repose beside the small, stockinged feet.

REBUILT LOST PARTS

"I rebuilt the lost parts, bandaged the broken parts and destroyed parts, which had to come out, I replaced. I put sufficient absorbent material for packing to soak her in solutions to feed her and develop the tissues, I made these solutions very carefully."

Harris asked him:

"Did you have the idea her spirit would unite with her body and commune with you?"

"And so it did," was the reply. "Many times she gave me advice, even technical advice, about the organ. When I don't know what to do next in repairing it, she tells me."

ASKED TO HIDE BODY

"She told me this trouble was coming. She asked me to hide her. I asked her what for. In a week's time trouble came. I knew while she was talking she did not want to tell me the details....

"I promised her I would keep and protect her the rest of my life, even with my own life, against destruction."

All who saw her agreed, Elena was a spectacularly beautiful young woman. Dressed in a "flapper" style dress with "costume" pearls and a rose in her hair, she may well have been on her way to a dance at the Cuban Club on Duval Street.

Elena and Luis Mesa on their wedding day.

Unable to live up to his vows to honor and cherish in sickness and in health, Luis Mesa abandonned his tragically ill wife as her condition worsened.

Key West, in the late 1920s, was a sleepy, remote town that never could have suspected von Cosel's obsession.

Von Cosel was employed as an X-ray technician at the Marine Hospital in Key West. It was here that he X-rayed Elena Mesa.

The mausoleum, surrounded by pine and palm trees, "looked more like a summer residence than a burial place, and it really was for my dear bride," recalled Count von Cosel.

The tombstone that adorned the right side of the mausoleum was a curious piece of work. Because von Cosel had paid for everything, his name was inscribed in the lower right hand corner.

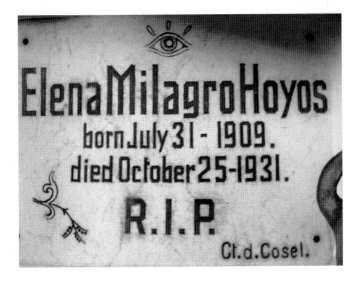

This was Elena's "castle" on Rest Beach. The hangar is at the far left and the tin roofing sheets were the hangar doors von Cosel described so vividly. His laboratory was in the enclosed area to the right.

"Airship Cts. Elaine von Cosel C-3" was Elena's home after their great escape from the mausoluem.

This photo most probably was taken by the Count. Only he knew that Elena was merely resting beside the little Christmas tree.

A caption on the original photo says, "Elena in her bed after resurrection."

Von Cosel stands proudly beside the equipment inside his laboratory. To the left is the million-volt transformer complete with ultra-violet and X-ray attachments.

The "incubator tank" that looks similar to a coffin is secured by padlocks.

The Count converses with Dr. DePoo (in the pinstriped suit), and attorney Louis Harris (seated). The pipe organ von Cosel was restoring provided a fitting backdrop.

Curious people (above) look at the Count's home on Flagler where he brought Elena's sister to show her how beautiful she was, leading to his arrest. As the sheriff took him away, he saw his Elena for the last time. She was removed from the house in a wicker basket by the undertaker.

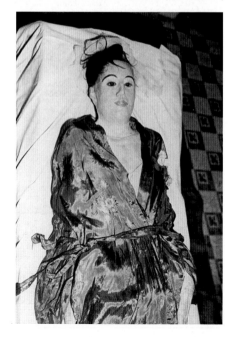

Elena rests peacefully on a bier at her second viewing inside the Lopez Funeral Home. The blue silk kimono complemented her rosy lips and glass eyes.

Looking more concerned about his appearance than his fate, the dapper Count speaks to court house onlookers.

The courtroom was as bizarre as the events that led up to it. The Count was dressed for the occasion—in black pants, white shirt, bow tie, tuxedo jacket and tennis shoes without socks.

The woman at the far left is probably Nana Medina, Elena's sister. The woman taking notes at the long table may be Jeanne Bellamy, the *Miami Herald* ace reporter.

Over 6,850 people attended her second viewing at the Lopez Funeral Home. It was suggested that Elena be put in a glass case like "Sleeping Beauty" as a tourist attraction.

Carl Tanzler von Cosel's memoirs eventually were published by a magazine called *Fantastic Adventures*.

The abridged story, "The Secret of Elena's Tomb," with illustrations, appeared in 1947, five years before the Count's death.

The chief witness against him was Mrs. Mario Medina, Elena's sister, and the closest relative still living.

At the end of the hearing, the same reporter, one of the first female reporters to be employed by a major newspaper, wrote an epitaph.

HEARING HELD FOR VON COSEL
ELDERLY ECENTRIC ORDERED RETURNED TO
JAIL AFTER TESTIFYING
By Jeanne Bellamy
Miami Herald Staff Writer

KEY WEST, Fla., Oct. 8—Carl Tanzler von Cosel was sent back to jail Tuesday under $1,000 bond after Enrique Esquinaldo, Peace Justice, took under advisement the testimony given at a three-hour hearing on charges that von Cosel had stolen the body of Elena Hoyos Mesa and kept it at his home for seven years.

"I know she is always with me. She is with me in this jail," said the white-bearded prisoner.

He testified for half an hour telling of his love for the young woman before she died of tuberculosis October 25, 1931. He had hoped to restore her to life and lavished tender care on the preserved dead body during the seven years he kept her in his home.

Von Cosel covered the decaying flesh with plaster of paris and wax, reconstructing the corpse into a startling resemblance of the young matron who was his obsession. The wax-covered skeleton was covered with a rich robe, and there was an artificial rose in the hair when officers invaded von Cosel's meager quarters and made the startling find.

More than 5,000 persons viewed the wax image Tuesday at the Lopez Funeral Home.

HOPED TO RESTORE LIFE

Von Cosel, German scientist, is the possessor of nine college degrees and was an X-ray expert. He hoped to use electrical rays to restore his sleeping beauty to life.

Allen B. Cleare Jr., county solicitor, said after the hearing that he would ask Raymond Lord, county judge, to appoint a lunacy commission.

"It is my opinion as a layman and with little knowledge of psychology that von Cosel has a mental quirk as far as this particular case is concerned," Cleare said.

The solicitor admitted, however, that he was convinced that on all other subjects von Cosel was normal. "He is an intelligent man, but his love for the girl has evidently got the best of him," Cleare said.

CONDITION SEEN AS OBSESSION

A widely known physician and surgeon, who has given some study to psychiatry and who did not desire his name to enter the case for business reasons, told the *Herald* that from what he had read of the account it is possible that von Cosel's case can be classed as on "the borderline state, characterized by certain obsessions, with other actions normal."

The physician cited the case of a kleptomaniac who might be wealthy, but would steal a five-cent handkerchief from a department store in explaining what he meant by the "borderline state."

Those who have occasion to talk to the old man declare that he is not insane. As a matter of fact, they have marveled at his intelligence. His knowledge of engineering, botany, art, medicine, and aviation is learned."

AGREE ON OBSESSION

That a man who would sleep beside the remains of a dead person for seven years is obsessed with a devotion that is stronger than the normal human, some will agree....

Authorities, who have come to like the kind man who wears a Van Dyke beard, have not made known the determination of the sister, Mrs. Mario Medina....

Von Cosel ate heartily Tuesday for the first time since he was arrested Saturday night. He changed from the party-soiled white duck pants and white shirt he wore when arrested to a serge suit and was anxious for the hearing.

The next evening, locals read yet another headline: October 9, 1940, the *Key West Citizen:*

ESQUINALDO DEFERS HEARING DECISION

VON COSEL RETURNED TO JAIL ON ORIGINAL
BOND; SESSION LASTED THREE HOURS

Carl Tanzler von Cosel was still confined in jail on the original bond of $1,000 set by Peace Justice Enrique Esquinaldo, Jr., Sunday, following the three-hour hearing held yesterday afternoon and evening at the county courthouse. The hearing was scheduled to determine whether the scientist should be held for Criminal Court trial on charge of violating a cemetery vault and removing the dead body of his sweetheart, Elena Hoyos Mesa.

Justice Esquinaldo indicated at the end of the hearing, which lasted from 5:30 to shortly before 9:00 last evening, that he would take the case under advisement for a few days and then make known his decision.

Hundreds of Key Westers and visitors strove to gain admittance to the chamber in which the hearing was conducted yesterday, but many were denied the privilege. All present listened with awe as von Cosel related in a low, steady voice, the strange story of how he had attended his sweetheart during her fatal illness and promised her the day before she died that he "would take care of her no matter what happened."

The chief witness appearing against him was the dead girl's sister, Mrs. Mario Medina.... The warrant, she explained, was sworn out after a weeks period of grace, and refusal of the scientist to return his sweetheart to the vault.

Officials of the cemetery, Mrs. William Sawyer, custodian, and Otto Bethel, sexton, reported on the broken vault door and Reggie Pritchard, local mortician, told of the original burial and disinterment for removal to the vault.

Following the hearing, many observers were of the opinion that no trial would be held, rather that the defendant would be ordered confined to a sanitarium. This Mr. Esquinaldo refused to comment on.

Authorities were investigating other angles of the case today in an effort to determine if others, besides the relatives and the defendant, were implicated in the strange case.

The press was having a field day.

On Wednesday morning, October 9, 1940, the *Miami Herald* headlines—above a photo of von Cosel, wearing a white suit jacket and holding an enlarged photograph of Elena—read:

SOUGHT TO BRING HER BACK TO LIFE
ECCENTRIC GAZES FONDLY AT PICTURE
OF DEAD SWEETHEART

The incredible story of a scientist, who for seven years has slept beside the dead body of the pretty young woman he loved, was unfolded at Key West. Here is Carl Tanzler von Cosel gazing affectionately at a picture of Mrs. Elena Hoyos Mesa, dead nine years, before he was taken to jail. He is charged with removing a body from its grave without permission. Below is the body of Mrs. Mesa, which von Cosel reconstructed with wax and paper maché "so I could have her with me always." At bottom is part of the 5,000 Key West residents who crowded the funeral home for a glimpse of the weird, lifelike corpse.

The day after the hearing, Judge Lord visited the Count in his cell and read the charges that were being considered. The obvious charge was, "the malicious and wanton disfigurement of a burial vault and the subsequent removal of the body without authorization." Judge Lord also informed von Cosel that he would not be allowed to see Elena and that she would not be returned to the vault he had built for her. Carl's heart physically ached when he learned that the new grave spoken about in the courtroom in which his beloved would be buried, would never be revealed to him. He would never be able to worship at the site where Elena was buried again.

"I was thunderstruck. This was not fair, this was monstrous. She to be buried again after all my work? Elena nothing to me? She, who was everything to me. All I could stammer was:

"It is the end of everything for me. I protest against this inhuman decision. You cannot do this. It means her utter ruin and a break of faith to my Elena. If I cannot have her back, I will abide by your decision, but I will carry on my fight to the highest court of the land to annul this decision."

NEWS OF INTERMENT SHAKES LOVER
SISTER ORDERS IMAGE TAKEN FROM VON COSEL

(Pictured directly under the bold headline were Nana Medina, sitting in a juror's chair wearing a distraught expression and von Cosel, also seated in a juror's chair, wearing the tuxedo. The photograph was taken moments before the hearing began.)

In spite of all the bizarre revelations, about Carl von Cosel's procedures to preserve the body (as well as the spirit) of Elena Hoyos, the public continued to rally to his side.

People from all over the country wrote in defense of von Cosel. The sympathy of thousands was stirred:

Will you please bring this letter to the attention of the proper authorities.

Relative to Carl Tanzler von Cosel, we feel that the very fact that he preserved a human body for the period of seven years is proof of his ability as a scientist; furthermore, his investigation into extreme research should be considered as a valuable human experimentation and not as a criminal case....

In these times, with the world's lust to kill and destroy, it is no more than expected for the mob to unjustly crucify— but if, by miracle, a person, such as professor von Cosel, could succeed in restoring to life a deceased person, the greatest discovery of all ages would have been made.

Even if the chances be a million to one against his chances of success, it was worth the try....

Past history reveals that most of our great scientists have been unjustly labeled by the majority who could neither follow nor comprehend, which, in reality, was an inner, hidden grudge against anyone who had the courage and intelligence to further the progress of the world....

We feel that not only should he be liberated, with compensation, but also, that he should be permitted to carry on with his subject with the permission of the subject's custodians.

Signed, Jack Hartman Linton and Mrs. Nettis Linton,

of Deerfield Beach, Florida, and Mrs. M. Sellman, of New York City.

As far as society failing to appreciate great scientists, the writers had a point. The man who discovered that yellow fever was carried by mosquitoes died the laughing stock of the medical community, who were certain the disease came from "bad air." Some people still have trouble with Darwin's theory of evolution.

In addition, there is little doubt that humanity, in general, wants a way to keep on living. That life ends, seems to symbolize the frustration mankind has over the finality of it all. As von Cosel would say, it's "metaphysical from every angle."

Looking into the future is always a guess, but there is the real possibility that science will discover the secrets of life and the aging process and that life will be greatly extended, perhaps indefinitely. Someday we may live happily or otherwise forever and ever after. The ramifications of that discovery are impossible to predict. However, in the present, life has a certain beginning and a terminal end. In such a setting, death makes life more intense. It creates urgency.

These sentiments were reflected in the press's treatment of von Cosel:

SCIENTIST'S FUTILE LOVE GAINS
SYMPATHY OF KEY WESTERS
By Jeanne Bellamy
Herald Staff Writer

KEY WEST, Fla., Oct. 9—Already the "love of von Cosel" has become a legend in this historic island city.

Public sympathy is overwhelmingly on the side of aged Carl Tanzler von Cosel, jailed since he admitted the life-sized doll enshrined in his dwelling for the past seven years was fashioned over the bones of Elena Hoyos Mesa, the beautiful young matron von Cosel adored before she died nine years ago.

"He hasn't done anything wrong," seems to be the unanimous opinion.

There is a feeling that the seventy-year-old scientist probably should be kept under observation for a check of his mental condition, but that he certainly does not deserve to be placed in a jail cell for any length of time.

EXALT OVER STORY

As a matter of fact, many eyes shine with a sort of exaltation during discussion of von Cosel's story.

Perhaps the marked Spanish strain in Key West's population has something to do with it.

It was in Spain that Don Quixote titled with windmills. And it was in Spain, long before, that the mummified body of the peerless warrior El Cid was brought from its resting place, seated on a giant horse and sent to lead wavering Spanish forces against the Moors, who were confounded by the apparition of the champion returned from death to conquer them again.

Like all events that capture public fancy, von Cosel's story is being embroidered fast.

IMAGINATION GETS PLAY

For instance, there is the tale, which proved purely imaginative, that he had strung telephone wires from his house to Elena's mausoleum so he could talk to her from afar on rainy days, before he took her bones home.

There is an ugly whisper purporting to be the "inside story" of why he kept Elena's effigy, but people refuse to believe that, preferring to think of him as a man crazed by the worship of his ideal beauty.

There is the rumor that federal agents were keeping close watch on his actions and had searched the crypt on the theory it might have contained radio equipment.

So strongly has von Cosel's dream clutched the imagination of Key West that a ballad titled "The Love of von Cosel" has been written by Orlando B. Esquinaldo, brother of the peace justice who conducted the hearing Tuesday on a warrant charging the bewhiskered old man with disturbing a grave and removing the contents.

He's still in jail, awaiting the magistrate's decision. Erect and courtly, he rises to greet visitors and chats amiably with them....

PACES IN SMALL CELL

Wednesday night, von Cosel was pacing the small cell in the county jail where he has been confined since his arrest

Sunday, unable to reconcile himself to the fact that he must part with Elena....

Von Cosel, who stole into the cemetery at night to take the remains of Elena from a crypt which he had built in order that he could "preserve and resurrect her," told the officials, "I will carry the fight to the highest courts in the land, if I live long enough, to obtain sufficient funds to regain her. She is mine. Her father gave her to me. I am more entitled to her than her sister."

HEARS LAW RECITED

Judge Lord read, for von Cosel's information, an excerpt from common law volume, which recites: "The unauthorized disinterring of the body of a deceased human being is an indictable offense, both at common law and by statute, regardless of the motive or purpose."

To this, von Cosel replied, "I might be in error for removing the body without permission of the health authorities, but that does not mean it is not mine to do with as I see best. Her father gave her to me."

Those who have known the scientist intimately scoff at the lunacy petition. "He will make monkeys out of them," one of the friends said. "He might be obsessed with the thought that he can bring life back to Elena. His love for her is responsible for this. He is not insane. Visit his home. See the electrical and engineering work he has done. View some of his paintings and his sculpture work and this will convince even the most persistent that this man is not insane."

And this seems to be the general opinion in Key West. That he has a strange mental quirk the residents will admit.

Meanwhile, the people of Key West took their places to see a sight they would never forget.

Once the sheriff had told Lopez Funeral Home to pick up Elena Hoyos's body, which they did in their funeral car, the question became what to do with it. Elena's remains didn't need either refrigeration or embalming.

A dispute arose over to whom the remains belonged. Elena and the funeral home were caught in the middle.

Nana wanted Elena's body buried. Von Cosel wanted her body

back. The law officials didn't want to have anything to do with the body. As for payment—von Cosel was in jail and her family had little money.

The funeral home, with little warning and no guidelines, was capriciously put in charge of a dead-for-nine-years celebrity. The morticians apparently decided to do what they usually did, put the deceased out for a "viewing."

For a person to have a second viewing nine years after the first was a curiosity, to say the least. The funeral home was the host, and Elena was the talk of the town. Hundreds of people wanted to see the bride of von Cosel. Never before had so many come to see the departed.

Despite the dire warning of a representative of the Catholic Church, few stayed away. Father Gallaghan warned the girls not to look at the body because it had received the sacraments and therefore, it was a "Temple of God that had been desecrated." He went on to say, "If von Cosel were to be judged by the Church he would have much to account for."

In fact, there were many kids, right up front gawking. The public schools, rumor has it, were let out to see what the press, both national and international, considered exceptionally newsworthy. So much for stern warnings. The pictures of the people looking at Elena and their expressions are a study. The atmosphere surrounding this true-life soap opera was described as "carnival-like." Even today, those children, now growing old, still have vivid recollections of seeing the body and the quirky von Cosel. Inevitably, they smile a mischievous smile and say, "All of us kids went down to see her."

The manager of the funeral home, who did the actual count, said 6,850 persons viewed the effigy.

"The body was put on exhibit. Put out for people to view it. It was at Lopez Funeral Home. Where the embalming room is now, it was just sitting inside. There was a doorway there and it was laying on a cot and they allowed people to walk by and look at it and what I remember of it to me, was a doll, a wax doll—very tiny and more like a child than an adult."

"Very lifelike though," said another woman.

A man who saw Elena was quoted as saying, "The hair was real, it was her own hair, but the rest of it was absolutely, positively, nothing but wax or something made out of cornstarch."

Another viewer claimed that the body felt soft, "just like if I touched your arm right now."

A more detail-conscious viewer said of Elena's ensemble, "She wore a cheap blue rayon robe. Her legs, quite full, were covered with heavy stockings. On her feet were cheap bedroom slippers. Her hands were covered with white gloves plastered down with wax. I couldn't help but notice protuberances of the hip bones."

THOUSANDS OF CURIOUS FILE PAST MAIDEN'S BIER

KEY WEST, Oct. 8—(AP)—The fantastic story of a man who sought to restore life to his loved one attracted thousands to an undertaking establishment for an awesome glimpse of the corpse which he kept in his bedroom for seven years....

[According to County Solicitor Cleare] he appears harmless and in fact, seems highly intelligent, but he doesn't know what would happen if the thread between obsession and insanity should snap.

"His existence has been woven around the memory of a girl for the last several years and no one knows how he will react if he feels he has lost the body forever...."

There were at least two people in Key West who had information about the "after life" relationship between Elena Hoyos and Carl von Cosel that both the press and the public would have found even more revealing—Doctor DePoo, who performed an autopsy on the body after it was discovered in von Cosel's home, and Dr. Foraker, who was in attendance—and they, for mysterious reasons, chose not to discuss the case until 1972, thirty-two years after the hearing.

Chapter Fourteen

Mad or Sane?

A lthough the public, especially its female members, clamored for von Cosel's acquittal, the question of the defendant's sanity still remained to be decided. An examination was to take place on Thursday, October 10th, two days after the hearing.

Von Cosel said, "I was called to the courthouse to be examined by three doctors, for sanity, by order of the court."

Any lawyer conscientiously representing the Count would have considered the defense of insanity as a way to vindicate or at least explain his behavior. Most crimes require that the defendant intends to break the law. The insane, legal logic goes, are incapable of the intent requirement and are therefore, not guilty. Attorney Harris could have influenced the sanity board had he felt it was the best approach, and he probably would have done so if the Count had allowed it. For von Cosel, it was totally out of the question, and he would have disassociated himself from anyone who favored this tactic because, for him, it was utterly false, completely untrue. Dr. von Cosel was not a nut; he was a great scientist, a visionary who was ahead of his time.

The press duly reported each nuance of the hearing. One poignant note was the letter from Doris Tanzler, von Cosel's forgotten wife:

VON COSEL'S WIFE COMMUNICATES
WITH OFFICER;
EXAMINATION LASTED AN HOUR
Deputy Sheriff Ray Elwood received a letter this noon from Mrs. Doris Tanzler, of Zephyrhills, Fla., claiming she is the wife of Carl Tanzler von Cosel. The letter read exactly as follows:

Dear Sir:

I note in the papers that Karl Tanzler is in custody.

He is my husband and we have been separated for eleven years. His mind is troubled on account of many ways. It was impossible for us to live together.

If my testimony as to his sanity is desirable, I will gladly tell all I know.

Sincerely,

Mrs. Doris Tanzler

Unmindful of her personal agony, the newspapers found Doris Tanzler an engrossing subject to fan the fires:

LOVER'S WIFE ENTERS BIZARRE CASE
WRITES FROM FLORIDA CITY
SHE'S READY TO TALK OF VON COSEL
By Earl Adams

KEY WEST, Fla., Oct. 10—The estranged wife of Carl Tanzler von Cosel said he left in Germany sixteen years ago turned up Thursday in Zephyrhills, Fla., ready to "tell what I know" about his sanity.

Her air mail letter reached Ray Elwood, deputy sheriff, a few hours after a court appointed lunacy board had certified as sane the scientist who kept the reconstructed body of a young matron in his bedroom for seven years.

SEPARATED IN GERMANY

Confronted with this letter, von Cosel read it through several times before saying:

"Sure, we separated. She was jealous. She pulled a gun on me. In the scuffle, a shot was fired. I decided then that I would leave her."

Von Cosel insisted that he separated from his wife in Dresden, Germany, sixteen years ago and that he had not heard from her in twelve years. Later he said that his sister, who resides in Zephyrhills, had written him that his wife was with her.

He has received no word from the sister since January, he said.

Asked for the name of the sister in Zephyrhills, von Cosel

said sharply, "Leave her out of this. I do not want her name to be brought into this. She is very old and sickly."

"Please get me some paper and an envelope," he asked Deputy Elwood. "I want to write my wife to keep out of this. I thought she had a divorce."

Doris Tanzler's letter revealed her strong depth of character despite an undeserved humiliation, an unimaginable nightmare-come-true. For the real Mrs. Tanzler, the hard-working, level-headed mother of their surviving daughter, had learned in the newspaper that her husband, the father of their child, not only had fallen in love with another woman, but had cared for Elena Hoyos's body rather than taking care of his true-life responsibilities.

Being abandoned was one thing, but having to endure the spectacle of Carl Tanzler was much worse. The curse of infamy and a feeling of guilt through marriage would follow and unfairly torment her for the rest of her life. From the day the articles began appearing in the newspapers, she would be known in Zephyrhills as the one who was married to the man who took the dead girl from the grave in Key West.

Doris Tanzler obviously wanted to testify, and why she wasn't summoned is another small mystery. What was surprising to those Key Westers who thought they knew Carl was that there existed a Mrs. Tanzler who was legally married to Mr. Tanzler, the same person calling himself Count Carl von Cosel, and that she was not living in Germany. She was living relatively close by in the state of Florida. Even more strange was that he failed to acknowledge his daughter.

The subject of Doris Tanzler came up in an interview with von Cosel written by Jeanne Bellamy, a *Miami Herald* reporter who diligently covered each new episode of the proceedings.

LIFE NEVER DEPARTS THE BODY
SO SAYS KEY WEST'S STRANGEST LOVER
CARL TANZLER VON COSEL
THE DEAD BUT SLEEP, HE SAYS
From a castle in Germany to a frame shack in Key West.
From opals, pipe organs, and a yacht to rusty screws, bed springs, pieces of wood, and a stuffed seagull.
From the study of calculus and metaphysics to concocted

solutions to restore life in a body nine years dead.

That is the story of Carl Tanzler von Cosel, as he himself told it in the county jail at Key West. He was placed there a week ago after he admitted the life-size figure he had kept in his bedroom for seven years was the body, reconstructed in wax, of twenty-two-year-old Elena Hoyos Mesa, the beautiful matron he fell in love with before she died in 1931.

His conviction that she can be brought back to life has aroused widespread controversy as to von Cosel's sanity.

Perhaps the answer lies in his own past, as he remembers it.

How much of this tale is fact, how much fantasy, the writer has no way of knowing....

"When I was a young fellow, I did not smoke. I did not drink. I did not go out dancing with the girls. I did not have time.

"I did fencing for exercise. That is a chivalrous art and exercises the whole body. It requires perfect coordination of mind and muscles."

Von Cosel became an engineer in Germany. He once patented an engineering device which he would not describe in detail.

"Someone tried to steal it from me. The lawyers took it to court but got nowhere, so I went into court and won the case myself. The government finally bought the patent."

He married and had "two lovely daughters," but his wife proved "war-like—quarrelsome, you would say," so they parted. He left them in Germany and has not heard from them for twelve years.

This part of his story was contradicted later when his wife turned up in Zephyrhills, Florida, saying they had separated only eleven years ago. His brief statement about the marriage and parting was in reply to a direct question, and von Cosel made no further mention of his wife. He said nothing about her being with him in Australia, although the time he fixed for separation—sixteen years ago—would have been after he left that continent.

In Australia, von Cosel said, he was employed by the government as an engineer.

"I had a beautiful residence overlooking the harbor at Sydney. I had a pipe organ, my boats, and a 125 foot-diesel-powered yacht, the *Aeyesha*. That is an Arabian name meaning, "The Star of the Heavens." There was a queen of that name in the Cocos Islands whose husband was an Englishman. She used to come to Sydney many times, and I saw that queen. She was Malayan with olive skin, loaded with diamonds, brilliants, and precious stones.

"I had the steel diesel motors of my yacht especially made in England so that it was very strong. I was building a seaplane with a 110-foot wing span and two 500-horse-power diesel engines. I became a licensed pilot, taking lessons from Monsieur Geau who brought seven planes from Paris.

"I left Australia after the World War. They made it so unpleasant for me. I had lived there for fifteen years, was a British citizen, a servant of the king. I was respected and had good friends everywhere, yet, as soon as the war broke out, they looked upon me as an enemy. The military moved me for my own safety, they said. They kept me in military headquarters for five years with several doctors, spies, and others.

"People broke into my residence about a hundred times and everyone went in and took what they liked. There were 100 windows and they were all broken. The inside was a shambles. The pipe organ was chopped to pieces with an ax. I lost my library, all my documents, my collection of diamonds, emeralds, and opals. I had some big ones, fiery opals as big as that."

He raised both hands and formed a circle about two inches in diameter with the spatulate fingers....

Von Cosel said he also owned an island coconut plantation as large as Key West near the equator, "near where Amelia Earhart went down."

"I still own it. I intend to go back when this war finishes and stay there several months."

In India, he came down with influenza and almost died.

"They had put me in the morgue. I heard a man's voice saying I was to be buried at five o'clock.

"That brought me back."

He came to the United States and was held at Ellis Island "for days" until his sister from Elizabeth, New Jersey, who wears the pants in her house, as they say, put up $20,000 bond for his admittance. He stayed in New York about one year, but "was glad to get away from there because I caught such a severe bronchitis in New York and was sick for months. It was too darn cold in the winter, colder than Germany."

He went back to Germany to see his mother, who was quite old.

"There was a revolution there at that time. The Russian soldiers—Communist bands—were roaming all over. They had robbed people on the streets of their clothes who had better than they had."

Apparently it was at this point that von Cosel left his wife and daughters in Dresden, making arrangements to provide for their financial needs from his German holdings. His friends in Key West said von Cosel used to receive from Germany regularly a monthly check for $150, but this sum dwindled after the Nazis came into power....

Asked if he believed there was still consciousness in Elena's body, von Cosel said:

"It is not the physical body. The physical body is asleep. The ears can hear, but the eyes cannot see because they are in darkness....

"That is the reason I placed Elena very close to the organ, so she could hear the music, heavenly music...."

The organ has not played for a year because von Cosel exchanged it for a larger one from a Negro church. This organ had been disabled for eight years, but von Cosel undertook the task of rebuilding it for Elena.

It stands amid great masses of junk in the open part of the abandoned building which has been von Cosel's home for the past several years.

In this most extensive interview conducted by Ms. Bellamy, von Cosel obviously needed little prodding to tell his side of the story. Perhaps the most truthful part of the article was the sentence that says, "How much of his tale is fact, how much fantasy, the writer has no way of knowing."

Members of the lunacy board did make it clear, however, that their decision had no bearing on von Cosel's guilt or innocence of the criminal charge of removing from a vault the remains of Elena Hoyos Mesa, and keeping them in his house....

It was not the sanity hearing, which he considered unimportant, but the reburial decision which concerned the Count.

"It was a far more miserable night than when she died," he said. "Then I knew it was God's wishes. This decision, however, to take her from me and bury her beneath the ground is the wish of man. What right have they?"

"Elena visited me in my cell just before sunlight broke through the window," he said. "She told me that I must get some sleep and not to worry any more. She knew that I desired so much to carry out my promise to be with her always. When she left I went to sleep."

With his usual military stance and quiet dignity, he emerged from the room after the sanity test.

Later in his cell, von Cosel remarked that they asked him scientific, medical and everyday questions. They asked him in particular about the antiseptic he used on Elena's body after he took it from the vault. He told them, he said: "Chinosol."

"How do you spell it?" they asked me. "I spelled it and told them that it was one of the most powerful germicides in the world and that I had ordered it from Hamburg, Germany. I paid $15 an ounce for it."

> **Visitors continued to call on me in the jail. They brought fruit and chocolate and the sweet Señorita Marguerita brought hot tea and biscuits for my supper in the evening again. And the invisible band still played that cradle song each night and I fell asleep.**

The doctors who examined von Cosel, despite the judgment of some outside experts, declared him to be sane. Of the hearing, he said:

> **There could be no other findings despite a few cranks who would like me declared insane.**

Once again, the press became frenzied. October 10, 1940, the *Key West Citizen:*

'HE'S SANE', DECLARED BOARD AFTER HEARING

Carl Tanzler von Cosel was adjudged sane today following a sanity hearing conducted in the sheriff's office.

Members of the sanity board were Dr. Wm. R. Warren, Dr. H. C. Galey, and Mrs. Gilmore Park, secretary to County Judge Raymond R. Lord. The hearing lasted a little over an hour.

Von Cosel, charged with the removal from the cemetery without proper permission of the remains of his dead sweetheart, Elena Hoyos Mesa, was not acquainted with this turn of events until this morning. Interested citizens had presented a petition to Judge Lord, who granted the hearing and named the board.

Disposition of the case now rests with Peace Justice Enrique Esquinaldo, Jr., who has yet to make known his decision as to whether von Cosel is to be held for Criminal Court trial on charges of violating state health laws.

Protesting threatened action which would deprive him of the wax and plaster of Paris remains of his sweetheart, von Cosel failed to show any violent reaction. County officials stated, however, that Circuit Court action would have to be taken before disposition of the remains could be determined.

A contradictory opinion as to the Count's sanity was offered in the *Miami Herald* by Dr. Ralph Green, medical director of Eastern Airlines:

VON COSEL MENTALLY ILL
OPINION OF MIAMI DOCTOR

"The macabre episode recently revealed in Key West is immediately suggestive that the living participant is of impaired mentality.

"From press notices which purport to accurately quote the elderly person involved, it is reasonable to assume that he is not the victim of senile deterioration because of his apparent ability in the realm of memory for recent events....

"A psychiatric conjectural opinion in a case of this kind under consideration would lead the expert to suspect a morbid mental trend technically known as 'necrophilism,; which term, reduced to understandable by lay language, is intended to mean the existence of insane love for dead bodies. In certain localities, morbid tendencies, particularly in the realm of acts of perversion, are classified as criminal offenses, punishable by imprisonment, usually not for a period longer than three years.

"It is difficult to understand how custodial treatment could correct mental disease. The logical disposition of a case of this kind is to regard the individual as mentally ill and entitled to benefits and kindly care of a well regulated hospital, wherein highly specialized skill in the treatment of mental disease is available.

"The outlook for recovery in cases of morbid practices is discouraging. However, under a well regulated institution or hospital regime, people thus afflicted are given the benefit of a kindly hospital atmosphere rather than the ill effects of a prison atmosphere amidst bolts and bars, a surrounding which is not conducive to peace of mind and hence is prejudicial to recovery."

When reflecting on the decisions being made, it's important to understand that every city official involved in the case was drifting into uncharted waters. Nothing remotely resembling von Cosel's love affair with the dead Elena Hoyos had ever happened before, so there was no precedent to follow.

The Count had lived in Key West for a number of years. If people didn't personally know him, they knew of him. Far from coming across as a quack who was mentally ill, he had been known as a dedicated, competent health-care professional who had, at one point in time or another, helped a great number of people. Mrs. Gilmore Park, who was at the sanity hearing as an official of the court, recently recounted that, although it was not her position to make the evaluation, she thought he was sane.

The magnifying glass of public scrutiny under which von Cosel was examined was large enough to encompass those empowered to dole out justice, and the strong breeze of public opinion was blowing the Count's way. He was charming, resolute, dignified, erect, scientific, and most importantly—he was an unearthly romantic:

> *He brought her flowers*
> *They were fresh every day*
> *He loved her so much*
> *And that's what flowers say*

Women especially were now united behind the Count, and everyone involved in the case was aware of it. Some men may have obscenely joked in private, as men sometimes do, about how to poke a pickled person, you've got to have a loose screw. They could laugh about how Elena didn't make him mow the lawn or care if he came home at dawn, but the men, too, were forgivingly nonjudgmental when it came to Carl von Cosel, who loved a woman so much he could not let her go.

WRITES POEM FOR VON COSEL
Editor, the Citizen:

Carl von Cosel is reputedly a poet. Will you please convey to him the poetic consultations of a kindred, though uncouth and exceedingly crude fellow poet.

If he desires, it can be published under the nom de plume of Red Bay Billie.

RED BAY BILLIE
Miami, Fla.,
October 9, 1940

TO ME SHE IS NOT DEAD, SHE BUT SLEEPETH
Love dieth not, though breath of life
From body shall depart,
And death's inevitable beckoning call
Doth still the beating heart
Aye, I wasn't lonely for thou
Though thou wasn't wafted hence,
And couldn'st thy body near me lie
 T'would be slight recompense
 Thus, in silence of the night,

No thought of man's laws breaking
I bore thee gently homeward
To still my sad heart's aching.
Thy spirit, smiling through the years
Through midnight's darkest gloom
Dids't hover round in mystic love
And cheer my lonely room
In life, in death, beloved the while,
And now in dastard durance vile
I like a prisoner for thy sake
'Cause I thy deceased frame did'st take
And sought with wax, to mould to make—
Perpetuate for love's own sake—thy smile
Ah, yes, men's stringent law I break;
They call me mad—for this mistake
But o'er again love for thy sake
Ten thousand prison years I'd take
Mock not, nor scoff, ye callous soul,
Think me not vile, a doddering ghoul,
Because for love—my love I stole,
With science sought to make her whole
Lord this I pray, be it thy will,
stretch forth thy hand and keep me 'till
Dark Shadowy death and Jordan past,
My inseparable love I find at last

              RED BAY BILLY

Not everyone, however, felt that von Cosel was a misbegotten romantic.

The headlines of the November 2, 1940, edition of *Miami Life,* a scandalous daily enthusiastically read:

KEY WESTER USED 'BODY' TO
GRATIFY SEX PASSION

You have heard in the Miami paper the unusual tale of the Key West "lover" who stole the "body" of his sweetheart, "reconstructed" it, and kept it in his home for seven years until discovered recently, when he was arrested upon a minor charge and then released on bond.

These papers, especially the *Miami Herald,* have probably caused you to sympathize with the crackpot "scientist."

You may even, like some, have hotly demanded that man
be given back the "body," and that he somehow be allowed
to live out his "idyll" with it.

If you feel aforesaid sympathy, *Miami Life*'s advice to
you is to avoid Key West. For there you'll be disillusioned,
startled, disgusted by the real truth.

You'll come to hate Carl Tanzler von Cosel, and look
upon him as a dangerous criminal whose sex obsessions
may break forth more revolting at any time....

Nana Medina, earnest and attractive, didn't know the
true status of the relations of Carl with her dead sister's
bones until some time after the story "broke." Then she
heard an ugly piece of gossip. Her first reaction was to in-
dignantly forbid any further exhibition of the "body," which
up to that time had been Key West's biggest tourist drawing
card, being shown covered as it was when first discovered
in Tanzler's double bed.... Then she determined to examine
the "body" more closely.

Up to this time, Mrs. Medina, while heartbroken over
what had happened to her sister's remains, couldn't feel too
angry at the man whom she believed to be the victim of senile and maudlin sentimentally. Now she suddenly saw him
in a different light. The story she heard was horrifying.

At the morgue she removed the covering from the effigy.
Its thin legs wore tan silk stockings.

The "body"—although not actually resembling a body at
all, and yet did not have the finished look of a wax figure—
was bedecked with jewelry, even including a wrist watch;
had silken shoes, and wore a boutonniere at one shoulder.

Why, to give impetus to his crazed imagination, Carl had
one arm so hinged and attached to the body that he might
have it clasp him in embrace!

Impossible you say?

Well, if you're sincerely in search of the truth, you'll find
Mr. and Mrs. Medina not only willing, but eager to convince
you.

The Medinas have convinced Key West!

What should immediately focus the attention of the state of Florida upon Key West, as well as Uncle Sam's, is the fact that this German subject is a potential murderer.

He is criminally insane.

He demonstrated dangerous cupidity in acquiring the bones of the pretty girl. For what purpose? The evidence offered by the effigy he manufactured with cloth, wax, hair, and what-not, is damning proof of his perversion, of his unspeakable intentions toward the bones of a girl for whom he professed love.

A degenerate like this German grows progressively worse, as any good alienist would testify.

His next step might be murder for the sake of acquiring another body upon which he might satiate his unearthly and abnormal desires.

Von Cosel should be put away by American authorities— or deported. The latter probably would be the best punishment that could be given him.

Not knowing exactly what to do, no official wanted to come down too harshly on the Count and risk the fall-out. In the case of von Cosel, the political side-step seemed like the best thing to do.

"He's sane," there was no need to bother Mrs. Doris Tanzler who would only complicate an already awkward situation. Likewise, no one was very anxious to find out whether the doctors examining her body had discovered anything unusual. They took the easy way out—the path of least resistance—because they wanted to be rid of this stranger-than-fiction, unbelievable, hot potato they were juggling amongst themselves.

Now all that remained was for the criminal court, with Judge William V. Albury on the bench, to convene on November 11th. Allen B. Cleare Jr., who conducted the investigation for the state at the hearing was scheduled to prosecute von Cosel.

Chapter Fifteen
Friends to the Rescue

Though the matter of his mental condition had been disposed of by the three people who had judged Carl von Cosel sane, there still remained other charges to be ruled upon.

On October 11th, the *Miami Herald* announced:

TRIAL ORDERED FOR VON COSEL
FACE CHARGE OF MOVING CORPSE
By Earl Adams
Herald Staff Writer

Key West, Oct. 11—Carl Tanzler von Cosel, German scientist, must stand trial in criminal court before a jury of six men for removing the corpse of Elena Hoyos Mesa and keeping her reconstructed remains for seven years.

[Peace Justice] Esquinaldo held the old scientist on the charge that he "did wantonly and maliciously disturb the contents of a certain tomb and grave."

Commenting on the contention of Defense Counsel Louis A. Harris, that the stature of limitations should be considered, Esquinaldo said that it was his opinion that the possession of the body for seven years was a continued violation of the law.

COURT TO CONVENE NOVEMBER 11

Criminal court, with Judge William Albury on the bench, is scheduled to convene November 11. Allen B. Cleare, who conducted the investigation for the state at the hearing, will prosecute von Cosel.

Dr. William R. Warren, city health officer, and Dr. Harry C. Galey, who found the aged lover sane, received permission from Esquinaldo to examine the effigy Friday. The physicians refused comment on their findings.

Asked if the physicians had given him a report on their examination, Esquinaldo said he had been informed by Dr. Warren that Elena's skeleton was the foundation around which the wax figure had been modeled. The bones, some decayed and others still decaying, were wrapped with gauze bandages and other absorbent material.

Von Cosel still remained in jail Friday night. Friends say they would post bond Saturday.

The *Miami Herald,* October 12:

GRAVE ROBBER TO FACE TRIAL
CHARGES TO BE AIRED IN CRIMINAL COURT AT
NOVEMBER TERM
KEY WEST, Oct. 12—(UP)—On a charge of "maliciously disturbing the contents of a grave," Carl Tanzler von Cosel … was held today for criminal court action.

Meanwhile, two Key West citizens, Benny Fernandez, who owned the New York Busy Bee Barbecue Stand and Joe Zorsky, the proprietor of the Cactus Garden Tourist Camp, came to von Cosel's aid:

CARL VON COSEL FREED FROM JAIL;
BOND POSTED
PEACE JUSTICE ESQUINALDO ORDERS SCIENTIST
HELD FOR NEXT SESSION OF CRIMINAL COURT
Carl Tanzler von Cosel was freed from his prison cell shortly after noon today, as two citizens of Key West posted property sufficient to cover the $1,000 bond which had been set at the time of his original arrest last Sunday.

Action to free the scientist was started this morning by Benjamin Fernandez and Joseph Zorsky, following the decision handed down yesterday by Peace Justice Enrique Esquinaldo, Jr., which bound von Cosel over for the Criminal Court session in November, on the second of two counts filed against him, which referred to "malicious and wanton violation of a cemetery vault."

Fernandez and Zorsky told the court:

"Persons in Key West who recall the circumstances surrounding Dr. von Cosel's kindly administrations while Elena Hoyos Mesa was in the hospital have implicit faith in his motives.

"In appreciation of the services he rendered then, for his devotion to the girl he loved, and in behalf of the humanitarian aspects of this present case, I have followed my best judgment in assisting in furnishing bond for the defendant. We who know him think he should be freed of all charges."

A short while later, von Cosel was called to the sheriff's office and notified that his bail had been posted.

I was free now. All I wanted was to go home. But my friends, Zorsky and Benny, would not let me go. Their car was waiting outside to take me to their hotel, the Cactus Terrace, where I was invited to stay as their guest and recuperate a while, for I needed the rest. They all tried to cheer me up and they protected me from curiosity. Many tried to see me by all kinds of maneuvers, but in vain. I had enough cross examination and was tired of it. I sorely needed rest though I never refused friendly conversation with honest people or with scientists.

The incarceration and the strain of the hearing were stressful enough, but it was the announcement before the sanity hearing that had most dispirited von Cosel. It was then that he had learned he would never see Elena again. The loss of his re-awakened love, his constant companion, was worse than the day she died. At least that decision had been God's, while the reburial was the wish of his adversary, Nana Medina.

Nana had not given up the fight to have von Cosel found guilty of stealing her sister's body from its tomb.

ELENA'S SISTER WANTS VON COSEL PUNISHED
by Earl Adams
Herald Staff Writer
Key West, Fla. Oct. 20—This is Nana Medina's answer to those who say the reconstructed body of her sister, Elena Hoyos Mesa, should be returned to Carl von Cosel, the Ger-

man scientist who kept it in his bedroom for seven years:

"Would your sentiments be the same if the body was that of one of your loved ones?"

With all the intensity of her Cuban ancestry, young Mrs. Medina is determined to see to it that von Cosel is punished for what she considers "one of the most outrageous crimes this world has ever known."

"He's no idealist. Instead of being lauded, he should be condemned," she declared.

ONLY CLOSE RELATIVE

She is the only close relative now living in Key West of the beautiful young matron who died nine years ago and whose remains were taken two years later to von Cosel's dwelling. Both parents died a few years after Elena.

"Von Cosel is guilty of the most heinous crime," is Mrs. Medina's conviction. "He should be put away.

"Would a sane man sleep beside an effigy for seven years? Why is it that the doctors who examined the wax image did not make public their findings? I understand that the two doctors who declared him sane later examined the body. I wonder if their opinion is the same since the thorough examination of the body."

SIGNED AFFIDAVIT

It was Mrs. Medina who signed the affidavit for the warrant that resulted in von Cosel's arrest for October 6....

"I am convinced that the man was driven insane by his desire for Elena," said Mrs. Medina. "He could not have her in life so he stole her body and imaged her to the best of his ability.

"It is hard to conceive, but I am firmly convinced that his removal of the body was not motivated by a desire to restore life, but was the act of a man driven insane by his love for Elena...."

Nana's pent-up emotions exploded:

"I will start from the beginning and tell the true story of how Elena came to meet the old man who has brought so much unpleasantness to me."

MET AT HOSPITAL

"He met my sister when she went to the hospital, where

he was then employed, to have some X-rays made. Her husband paid for the X-rays. After she returned to our home, von Cosel asked permission to call, saying he was interested in Elena's illness from a medical standpoint. He wanted to treat my sister with a machine he had, but she and my parents objected because he was not a doctor.

"He would pester my sister about marrying him. He became so persistent that we asked him to stay away from the house. He did remain away for several months and then one day he returned. He started bringing my sister gifts. He gave her a ring, wrist watch, and some bar pins worth about $600.

"During the time my father ordered him to remain away from our home, he wrote a letter to my father in which he stated, if a wedding did not occur in our family before Christmas, that there would be a funeral."

RENTED HER ROOM

"On the day Elena died he arrived at the house shortly after her death. He had an ultra-violet ray machine which he used on her for a few minutes before our family physician arrived and pronounced Elena dead. He desired to continue working on the body insisting he could restore life, but my father refused.

"After Elena's death, on his urgent request, we rented him the room that she had occupied for $5 a month. We had to furnish him with tea, toast, scrambled eggs, and fish for his small payment and he never did pay us promptly.

"Came the day he lost his job at the hospital. He engaged my husband to drive a truck which towed his airplane to the building on Rest Beach where he was to live. Elena's body was transported in the cabin of the plane," he testified at the hearing.

FATHER RODE ON TRUCK

"They drove by my home and I was sitting on the porch with my father and mother. Little did we realize that Elena's body was in that plane. My father accepted an invitation from von Cosel to ride on the truck.

"He states that my father gave him Elena's body. That is an untruth. He asked father, could he have the body disin-

terred and placed in a vault, and my father, after consulting
with my mother, granted that permission. If father gave permission to do with the body as he saw fit, why did he not tell
my father the day he moved the body in the plane that it was
there?

"He asked for, and was given, all the jewelry and even
the bed that he bought for Elena."

Despite Nana's words about the gifts, von Cosel battled over
Elena's jewelry and won.

VON COSEL GETS ELENA'S JEWELRY
CALLED AT COURTHOUSE YESTERDAY MORNING;
CURIOUS CROWDS IN CITY
Dr. Carl Tanzler von Cosel visited the sheriff's office yesterday morning and received the jewels that had been worn
by his dead sweetheart, Elena Hoyos Mesa. The jewels, it is
revealed, had been given to the dead girl before she died
over nine years ago, and legally belonged to von Cosel....

Legally, the gifts the Count gave to Elena before her death became her property when she accepted them. Unless she willed them
to him (no mention of a last will and testament was made), they
should have become the property of her descendants by the laws
governing intestate (when there is no will) distribution. Simply put,
Nana, as the sole surviving family member, should have been entitled to the before-death gifts.

Not so, however, if the gifts were given to Elena after her death
because acceptance is one of the requirements of gift giving and re-
ceiving. In the law's eyes, a dead person can't say "thank you" or
"no thank you," so any jewelry von Cosel gave to Elena after her
death would still belong to him, the giver.

Despite the comfort of the hotel to which his kind friends had
taken him, the mysterious force of his departed beckoned the Count
home again.

But all the time I was pining to be back in the room again,
where Elena's bed stood, despite the excellent comforts here
in the hotel and the kind hospitality. There was a mysterious

force, it was Elena herself, which urged me to come back to where she had been with me. So, on October 19, I went home to take charge of my premises and give Frank, who had been guarding the place day and night, a well deserved rest. There I found, in the meantime, that almost half of my dogs had died, amongst them 'Granny,' my good, old faithful Granny.

The *Citizen* reported the homage:

DR. VON COSEL'S CASE RECEIVES INCREASING NATIONAL INTEREST

Continued and increasing interest in Dr. Carl Tanzler von Cosel's unusual case, which now awaits trial in the November term of Criminal Court, has been evidenced in all parts of the nation. Letters arrive from many sections addressed not only to Dr. von Cosel, but to all other principals in the sensational and fantastic revelations recently disclosed.

Dr. von Cosel together with one of his bondsmen, Joseph Zorsky, called at the *Citizen* office this noon, for an informal talk on some aspects of the case. Three letters received, all expressing sympathy for the defendant, were read and discussed. Other letters, von Cosel stated, were being received in each mail.

As a small child, I loved to be with the young lady in my mother's art needlework shop. She told me beautiful stories; the one I loved best was about The Sleeping Beauty. She lay in a glass case breathing ever so gently at Madame Tressard's, London, England.

What on earth could be wrong in placing Dr. von Cosel's 'Sleeping Beauty' in an airtight, glass case? She belongs to him absolutely. Is it not wonderful in this world today to find such a kindly thought?

I have enclosed one dollar towards purchase of such a glass case."

CLARA MASON, *Hollywood, Calif.*

The *Miami Herald* and the *Key West Citizen* were not the only newspapers covering the love affair that people couldn't resist reading about. The Associated Press wire service carried the story to every paper in the country. Native Key West Resident, Bascom Grooms, was stationed in Los Angeles, California, when the story appeared on the front page of the *L.A. Times*. He became a celebrity of sorts because he actually, personally, knew the:

MAN WHO KEPT GIRL'S BODY IN WAX
SAYS HE HAD HOPED TO RESTORE LIFE

KEY WEST, Fla., Oct. 7—(AP)—Police pieced together today the strange story of a man they accused of keeping in his bedroom for seven years the preserved body of a young woman whom he hoped to restore to life.

The man, a medical expert in X-ray holding degrees from Leipzig University in Germany, was booked as Carl Tanzler Van Cosel and was charged with removing the body from its grave without permission.

Van Cosel was quoted by Deputy Sheriff Elwood:

"I did not want one so beautiful to go to dust."

"I tried experiments to restore her to life," his story continued, "I hope still if I live long enough to bring her back...."

Friends of Elena recalled Monday that one of her favorite songs was the Spanish song "Bodas Negros," the lyrics of which tells of a "lover stealing into a cemetery on a stormy night to steal the remains of his dead sweetheart and how he carried his beloved to his room, and laying her on his bed, covered her with flowers, lay beside her, and committed suicide...."

The article went on to tell the rest of the story, which was at the time titillating the entire nation's imagination. If it hadn't been for the photographs, people would not have believed it actually happened.

But, the supreme prize for capitalization and creativity went to Cuba, the island on which Count con Cosel had originally looked unsuccessfully for the dark-eyed beauty promised to him by ghostly apparitions.

Havana radio station CMQ began running a nightly "novela," a soap opera, based on the super-sensational affair. Each emotional episode was anxiously awaited by a huge audience glued to their radio sets. Listeners on both sides of the Florida Straits were hungry for the next installment that loosely chronicled what had taken place. The theme song for the novela was, but of course, "La Bode Negra," the black wedding. It was only fitting.

The show caused such a sensation that the Cuban government actually forced it off the air and sent a delegation aboard the S.S. *Cuba* to investigate the curious goings-on ninety miles north of Havana.

CUBAN OFFICIALS VISIT CITY ON VON COSEL CASE
INTEREST IN CUBA AROUSED TO HIGH PITCH;
BROADCASTS STOPPED UNTIL CASE IS
INVESTIGATED

By order of the Cuban Department of Justice, two Cuban visitors, each representing the two sides of the controversial von Cosel case, will arrive in Key West tomorrow afternoon aboard the S.S. *Cuba,* to conduct an investigation of the case. Interest has run continually high in Cuba, with broadcasting stations featuring special ... dramas almost nightly since the facts broke into public attention on Sunday, October 6.

With the realization that the case has "two sides," Cuban officials have ordered all broadcasts stopped until a check could be made on later angles now developing.

The two lawyers who will arrive here tomorrow are Dr. C. M. Palma, famous criminal lawyer in Havana, and Miss Margarita Pinto.

A large delegation of Key West's Cuban colony plans to welcome the visitors tomorrow, it is stated.

After docking at the Key West Harbor on October 22, 1940, the delegation learned from reading the *Miami Herald* the answer to the question people all over were waiting to find out:

VON COSEL WILL NOT BE PUNISHED

The Monroe County grand jury decided Saturday that von Cosel cannot be prosecuted now, even if he committed a crime by taking the body seven years ago.

Then, the County Solicitor, Allen B. Cleare, Jr., made his

announcement to Albury, telling him the X-ray technician would not be tried for removing the body of Elena Hoyos Mesa from the crypt he had built for it.

"I can find no law under which von Cosel can be tried which is not barred by the statute of limitations," Cleare reported.

Cleare directed the remains to be returned to the dead woman's sister, Mrs. Nana Medina, who said the body will be buried.

In hushed whispers, in laughing banter, in serious discussions, every raw happening in the court case was commented upon and debated. Some knowledgeable in legal matters questioned the application of the statute of limitations with regard to the "destroying the grave" charges. Most laws have time periods within which charges must be brought. Two years was the statutory limitation for molesting a grave, and Elena had been with the Count for seven years.

As for the "unauthorized disinterring of a body," it seems the judge decided to just let it go. Realistically, they could have easily brought von Cosel to trial had they wanted to. There were plenty of charges and sufficient evidence that could have been used against him—especially in light of what Dr. DePoo had found out, although there is no way of being certain he shared this information with the judge. Judge Lord apparently decided that justice would best be served if the whole thing was dropped and Elena's body buried where the Count couldn't find her. It's safe to say this was a trial the judicial system was trying its hardest to avoid.

There were some interesting, confusing, and arguable legal defenses available to von Cosel that Attorney Harris might have raised had the case gone to trial. At what point in time is it permissible to take a "mummy" from its grave? Elena was not an ancient Egyptian princess, but based on her appearance at the second viewing, she was far from her "natural" state.

Though a poor legal argument because a crime is generally a violation of a state statute, the issue of "consent" could have been a good legal side-show. Was it possible that the Hoyos family knew what the Count had done? An article entitled "Police Officer Bienvenido Perez Only Living Person Who Knows Where Elena Buried," raises that possibility:

"I believe that Elena was never put in that vault at all. It was probably that dummy he made of wax and plaster of Paris which they found over in Zephyrhills. He made a bust and a mask, modeling it while Elena was still alive. One reason was to fool her family so that if anyone saw the real body, he could substitute this image and say that is what they had seen. I think this is true because I saw the real body in the plane only five months after Elena died. I touched it, and it was soft, not just made of wax then. I told her family, but they did not believe me."

Perez was patrolling the area and was curious about the plane in the yard. Every time he approached it, von Cosel would get angry.

"One day he stuck his head out of the little window of the plane and yelled at me to stay away from the plane because it was charged with electricity. That made me suspicious more than ever. So soon after that, and this was about five months after Elena was supposedly buried the first time in a regular grave (and before the fancy tomb was built), I decided to investigate. I pulled a barrel over to the plane and stood up on it. When I looked in I saw something like a body all covered up. So I went inside the plane. There was the body all carefully ... waxed all around like a mummy but with the face showing. It scared me at first. He had put in big glass eyes wide open, and her black hair. It was easy to recognize Elena. There was no odor. I touched the arms and legs and they were soft under the wrapping, but the shoulders were dry like a mummy's."

Perez claimed that he contacted the sister, Mrs. Medina, and told her what he had found. She refused to believe Perez. She insisted on letting the matter drop.

Paul Vasquez, a Key West shell collector, commented:

"Von Cosel gave money to her family to keep their mouths shut. They knew all along he had Elena. But they did not believe that he abused her body in any way. They knew he adored her...."

In fact, under the circumstances, there was a good chance a jury of his peers would not have known what to think or believe at a trial.

Chapter Sixteen

Rest in Peace, Elena

The final disposition of Elena Hoyos was every bit as eerie and unconventional as von Cosel's behavior had been, because those responsible for her third trip to the cemetery didn't want the obsessed German Count to dig her up again. The solution proved that strange circumstances can produce equally strange and unusual results.

Three people were entrusted with Elena's burial: Key West Police Chief Bienvenido Perez, Lopez Funeral Home undertaker Benjamin Sawyer, and Cemetery Sexton Otto Bethel.

The official troika discussed at length how they should go about their task, and it was during these macabre discussions that they made a solemn promise to each other. Never, ever in their lifetime would they reveal the location of the grave.

In order to hide the burial, they dismembered Elena and put what was left of her into an eighteen-inch-square casket which could be buried secretly much more easily.

Later, Chief Perez recounted the harrowing night they smuggled Elena and the digging equipment into the cemetery:

> "Do you think that's deep enough?" I stepped back into the black pool of shadow under the quietly rustling palms and leaned on my shovel, looking inquiringly at undertaker Ben Sawyer and Sexton Bethel.
>
> The time was something after 3 a.m. on a dark summer morning. The place was a secluded spot in the Key West City Cemetery. And my mission was to bury, in a secret spot which could never be found, all that remained of the beautiful Elena Milagro Hoyos.
>
> "That'll do," Ben said laconically; but I knew his nerves

were about to snap, as mine were. For, another hour before, Ben and I had cut up with a hacksaw all that was left of the body of the beautiful Elena—which wasn't much—and packed the remains in a small specially made box, eighteen inches cubewise.

"All right, hand me the box," I ordered.

Bethel and Sawyer passed it to me. Carefully, gently, for she'd been my dear friend, I placed the small box containing Elena Hoyos in the shallow hole I'd dug. Then we filled it in, tamping the dirt down with infinite patience. After that we replaced the grass and other growth above the spot, until it was impossible to tell a hole had been dug. That was important, for no one must ever know the resting place of Elena Milagro Hoyos. And to this day, no one knows but me. Ben's dead. Bethel's dead. And the secret will go with me to my own grave.

Naturally there has been a lot of speculation as to the exact location of the grave. Most think Elena was buried somewhere in the old cemetery, but the feeling is not universal. Several old Conchs insist she was buried behind Key West's oldest home. They say the remains are under the brick fireplace. Others have insisted she was secretly buried behind the Catholic Church.

There is also speculation that she was buried close to the cemetery sexton's office so he could keep an eye on her.

Wherever she is, at the end of his life, Bienvenido Perez repeated his pledge of secrecy before he joined Ben and Bethel in the next world.

I believe he kept his promise.

Chapter Seventeen

Until We Meet Again

Dispirited and despairing, the lonely Count had lost the only thing meaningful to him.

> When in November, 1940, I was finally released from prison, I was a very bitter man. Charges had been brought against me that I was a violator of the grave, a ghoul, a fiend of society. There was an avalanche of misrepresentation, of sensational press stories which accused me of being a sexual pervert, a necromancer, a maniac, while being confined for court hearing. Worst of all, they had removed Elena's body, that body which I had treated, first to preserve it in its unearthly beauty, and then to reunite with its soul which always was with me in the scientific efforts of over seven years. What made these misfortunes even heavier was the fact that, at the time of my release, I had lost my employment through Roosevelt's entrenchment, had lost my home on the beach of Florida, which had been destroyed by hoodlums before my captivity, and with the war restrictions, found myself almost without means of existence.

So no one was more surprised than Carl von Cosel at the continued interest in and sympathy for him.

> By hundreds and thousands, people came to see me at my hermitage on Flagler Avenue. The license plates of their cars represented every state in the Union and there were visitors from the Bahamas, from Cuba, and from Canada. They were kindhearted people, all of them, and full of sympathy. It made me feel glad after this unpleasant experience. Folks came to

shake hands with me and to see the airplane and the organ, to take pictures and even movies in Technicolor. I took this as a homage for my darling Elena and it made me proud. Some asked for flowers, others took along some small discarded [presumably musical] organ parts. Ladies begged for tiny bits of Elena's bridal dress for a souvenir; even nails and screws of my laboratory were in demand. I hadn't thought I would like visitors, but as it turned out, they did me a lot of good.

Von Cosel, who had little money left, began charging a quarter a person for the grand tour, which included his own personal commentary. He badly needed the proceeds. A dollar would buy a week's supplies at one of the small grocery stores called "bodegas." For five dollars a month, you could rent a room that included breakfast.

Other than the money he received for the article he wrote and sold to the *Rosicrucian Digest* about building an organ from seacoast debris while in the Australian prison camp, the Count had no income. His dwindling monthly checks were no longer worth very much, probably due to the German mark's diminishing value.

However, because of the generosity of those who sympathized with him:

> Soon I was able to provide appropriate little gifts; pictures of Elena and some of the plaster of Paris death masks I had made for her.
> For months on end, this public interest set new records for traffic on the highways and on the toll bridges leading to Key West. People began to tell me that I had "put Key West on the map."

Though at first it pleased him, it was, in part, his notoriety in Key West that caused von Cosel to decide to leave. The move was an agonizing one. Key West had been his home for a long time. Key West had been Elena's home. The streets of Key West were where she had walked and talked with people. It was where she, alive, had taken her final automobile ride as well as her ninth and final postmortem journey. Von Cosel was also leaving the site of the Marine Hospital, where he first met Elena—leaving must have been very difficult.

But in Key West, he no longer had a life of his own. The Count had become a tourist attraction. He was always answering questions from yet another person with out-of-state license plates. He wanted to go someplace where he could write his memoirs. He was seeking seclusion. Granted, there was a lot of support for von Cosel, but it wasn't unanimous. The stress of notoriety and the fear that locals might have a change of heart if the whole story came out weighed heavily on the Count.

Moreover, he had little to live on, no job, and soon the adulation began to take its toll on the aging scientist.

> But although it was a pleasure and a comfort to me to find that I had so many friends, there was considerable physical strain involved in this. For they came as early as dawn and they kept coming till late at night. I hardly had any time to get a meal and they all wanted for me to tell the story; an impossible feat for me, since the complete story takes hours to tell. But then, I always did the best I could and it was because so many friendly people urged me to write a book so they could read and keep the story, that I promised them that I would do so when I would have time, but at present, I was much too busy.

Throughout the years, Carl had corresponded with his sister, who, still living in Zephyrhills, was having health problems and could use help. Zephyrhills was a small town in a sparsely populated rural part off the state, and the only other place in the United States with which Carl was even vaguely familiar. There too, for better or for worse, lived his wife, Doris, and their teenage daughter, but that didn't bother Carl Tanzler. It didn't occur to him that his presence in his real family's hometown would be difficult for them. He had somehow completely blocked their feelings from his conscience.

Von Cosel began making preparations and going through his earthly possessions, deciding what he must take and what had to be left behind. There was no question about certain things: Elena's casket, the wingless airplane, and the large organ he was restoring must go with him. He couldn't leave his organ behind because without it he wouldn't be able to play Wagner or Bach. Without his plane he wouldn't be able to fly back to Key West when the time was right, nor would he be able to feel Elena's presence.

In between visitors, he organized his possessions and took care of details like finding a trucking firm to transport his belongings.

For two hundred dollars, he hired three large trucks. The tail of the airplane stuck out of the back of the largest one. Piled high on either side of the fuselage and loaded into the remaining trucks was the organ and other indispensable things that the Count couldn't bear to leave behind. He carefully packed the coffin himself.

Von Cosel explained his impending departure by saying he needed to go some place where he could peacefully set the record straight and write his memoirs.

> With my whole life thus deranged, I lived for a time as a recluse amongst the rubble of my laboratory, using the airplane, which I had built for Elena, as a shelter. But then, a strange and unexpected turn of affairs brought me back to life. I discovered that there was human decency left in this world. From all parts of American and even from foreign countries, hundreds of letters poured in and thousands of visitors came to see me, not from idle curiosity, but from humane sympathy. In their eyes, I had not committed a crime. Gradually faith recovered and hope returned into my heart. I decided that it was my duty to answer comprehensively those thousands of questions I had been asked in connection with my life, and my love for Elena. I decided also that it was my duty to clear myself in the eyes of the public of the false accusations which had been raised. In short, I found it necessary to tell my story, to remove this spectre of ignorance.

His new celebrity status and the anxiety weren't the only things occupying von Cosel's mind and psyche. There was a tremendous undertow of indignation and downright anger flowing through his body.

When he thought of the absurdity of the charges they had tried to bring against him, "wanton and willful destruction of a tomb," it was so ludicrous it was laughable. This unjust charge was what ended everything for him, everything for which he had worked so hard. Now, he could never take Elena away in her airship, above the atmosphere all the way to heaven. Perhaps he'd show them what the "wanton and willful destruction of a tomb" really was!

No one was at von Cosel's home when he opened the locked box that contained the blasting caps, the clock, the battery, and most importantly, the dynamite. He went through a dress rehearsal, like the dress rehearsal he had before he rescued Elena from the mausoleum. Preparation, he knew from his scientific experiments, was the key to success.

Placing the test device he had made in an unpopulated area close enough to home so that he could hear it, but far enough away so as not to attract attention, he returned to his cabin and waited. He did not want to hurt anyone, that wasn't his goal. When the explosion occurred precisely as he had timed it, he knew he would go through with his plan.

The night before the caravan was to leave, dressed in the black suit he had worn when he visited the mausoleum, before Elena had come home with him, von Cosel walked in the dark shadows to the cemetery. Few saw him at two o'clock in the morning and the ones who did assumed he was merely on his way to the cemetery as he had been so many times in the past. Although he didn't know the location of Elena's new grave, he believed her spirit guided him as he walked purposefully down White Street, cutting over to Frances Street at Olivia Street. As the only one with a key to the stout mausoleum door, he was able to quietly slip inside.

There were so many memories, the most spectacular being the night the departed reached out of the ground and helped him and his love on their way to a new life. Tears rolled down von Cosel's cheeks as he took the sticks of dynamite out of his coat and wedged them above the wooden door jamb. The difficult part was to make the timer go off in twenty-four hours, not twelve. Hoping he hadn't been seen, he quietly locked the door, said his farewell and began walking for the last time back to Flagler Avenue in the darkness.

At home, in the bed where Elena had died and then come back to life, he rested his tired body for a few hours before the break of dawn.

There was so much to be done when he awoke at sunup that he was thoroughly exhausted when he and the truckers finally got underway early that evening.

He was in no mood for "funning" around when his entourage

stopped in front of Che Che's Bar on Division Street. It was late. The sun hadn't been down long. At Che Che's, a group of men started laughing at this procession with the airplane tail sticking out of the rear of one of the trucks. Derisively, they tied a "cubeta amarillo" chamber pot on the plane's tail which infuriated von Cosel.

Von Cosel was ready to start throwing punches until the men lightened up and invited him in for a drink, which he accepted before his long and sad journey began. Von Cosel left town at about nine o'clock in the evening on April 14, 1941. Six months from the day he had been released from jail after the hearing.

It was duly reported:

VON COSEL LEAVES HOME AT KEY WEST
UNABLE TO FIND PLACE TO LIVE,
GERMAN TO JOIN HIS SISTER
Herald Bureau

Key West, Fla., April 14—Ordered from the dilapidated shack that he occupied on the outskirts of this city, Carl Tanzler Von Cosel left Key West Monday night for Zephyrhills to make his home.

The German broke into the national limelight in October of last year when he was responsible for as bizarre a news story as 1940 recorded.

Arrested by county authorities for having stolen from a vault in the city cemetery the remains of nineteen-year-old Elena Hoyos Mesa, the aged German admitted having reconstructed the body with wax and plaster of Paris, smuggled it from place to place in an airplane and finally placing it in bed, beside which he slept nightly for seven years. He declared great love for the girl who prompted the act.

SKELETON ACT

Nothing remained of the young matron's body but the skeleton, but von Cosel, who is, among other things, a sculptor and painter, reconstructed so striking an image that it was first supposed that he had done an extraordinary job of embalming....

"I am going to my sister, who has a farm about three miles out from Zephyrhills," he said. "I cannot find a place here to stay and my sister is sick and alone."

After waving good-bye to his companions at the bar and some friends who had come to see him off, von Cosel, riding in the lead truck, began his trek up the Overseas Highway. Dressed in his black tuxedo with a bow tie, wearing his best fedora, he sat stoically silent, confident his departure would be remembered.

A few hours later, he was proved right.

The *Key West Citizen* headline read:

VON COSEL TOMB SMASHED BY EXPLOSION IN EARLY MORNING
BLAST OCCURRED FOUR HOURS AFTER AGED
SCIENTIST HAD LEFT KEY WEST LAST NIGHT

A violent explosion at 1:40 o'clock this morning smashed part of the tomb which Carl Tanzler Von Cosel built for the body of nineteen-year-old Elena Hoyos.

The explosion heard throughout the city occurred about four hours after the doctor and three moving vans bearing his personal possessions had rolled out of Key West.

The article speculated on the cause, and stated officials were at a loss to explain the blast. Police officers and the County Solicitor declined to say what, if any, action would be taken. They thought this might be an act of revenge by someone who disliked the Count, and they were partially correct.

The *Miami Herald* reported:

BLAST DESTROYS ELENA'S VAULT
WRECKED AFTER VON COSEL LEAVES KEY WEST
BELIEVE TWO STICKS OF DYNAMITE USED;
NO EVIDENCE OF BOMB
By Earl Adams
Manager, Herald Staff

Key West, Fla., April 15—The vault in the city cemetery from which Carl Tanzler von Cosel, emigrant from Germany, stole the remains of Elena Hoyos Mesa, Cuban matron, was mysteriously blown up at 1:45 a.m., Tuesday, little less than five hours after the eccentric German had left for Zephyrhills to make his home.

The front section of the vault was blown away by the explosion which aroused many Key West residents from their slumber.

Deputy Sheriff Frank Stickney and Otto Bethel, city sexton, said there was no evidence of a time bomb. Men familiar with the handling of dynamite told Stickney, he said, that at least two sticks of the explosive had been placed on top of the vault.

BUILT BY GERMAN

The mausoleum was built by von Cosel on ground purchased from the city after Elena's death.

Von Cosel left Key West shortly before 9 p.m., Tuesday, riding in an eight-ton van which carried his equipment and household furnishings. Another truck transported the airplane in which he moved Elena's body from place to place during his search for a permanent abode.

Before his departure Tuesday, von Cosel said that he was going to a farm owned by his sister near Zephyrhills. Asked if he would attempt reconciliation with the wife he married in Germany and later deserted, the aged German said he did not expect to see her, although he admitted she was in Zephyrhills.

FORCED TO SEEK CHARITY

Forced to seek charity when he was arrested last October for removing the Cuban matron's remains from the vault, von Cosel said Tuesday night that he was paying $200 to the trucking company to transport his belongings.

He made a tiny sum this past winter charging visitors a twenty-five-cent admission charge to his home. There he would tell the story of how he hoped to resurrect Elena and fly away with her in his airplane.

"I hate to leave Key West, for my Elena is buried here," he said. "But I will complete work on my plane some day and fly back here to her. She will be with me in spirit when I'm away," he declared.

Although a later newspaper article said that the sheriff and sexton had concluded von Cosel couldn't have been the culprit, everyone in town knew he was. The timing of the blast was too coincidental. If vandals had done it, they would have been found out. No, it was surely Count Carl von Cosel's "adieu."

And again, it was easier to let him go and not prosecute him for "the wanton and willful destruction of a tomb" after they had decided not to prosecute him for the "wanton and willful destruction of a tomb" that he had built and maintained, not wantonly and willfully destroyed in the first place. Wasn't this a "tomb" without a body in it? Didn't the Count own the mausoleum? Why couldn't he blow it up if that's the way he felt about things?

It was all too confusing and definitely more convenient to leave the mystery unsolved.

Chapter Eighteen

Carl Tanzler Returns to Zephyrhills

Through Big Pine, around the curve at Bahia Honda, and over the narrow Seven Mile Bridge constructed on the trusses where the Overseas Railroad had been five years earlier—all night long he rode in the truck over the roads that had replaced the train tracks in 1937. It was a lonely stretch in the darkness in 1940. He didn't see a car until he got to a little place called Marathon, fifty-five miles from Key West. The pungent salt air was sticky and smelled like the ocean until they passed Card Sound Road. Everything felt a little damp shortly before dawn.

Traveling east on highway A1A, looking directly into the sun as it rose, all were relieved when they took the turn northward at Homestead. Though it was warm, the breeze that came in through the open windows made it pleasant enough as they rode on the two-lane highway through sugar country and then orange groves.

He wouldn't buy the *Miami Herald* until reaching Zephyrhills because he didn't want to arouse the suspicion of the truck drivers who accompanied him. For all the Count knew, he might be a fugitive from justice, wanted for the destruction of a tomb that occurred well within the statute of limitations. When he found a paper and read the article by Earl Adams, the Count knew his plan had succeeded.

The satisfaction that came from reading about the explosion somewhat picked up his spirits. Earlier, he had felt extremely down as he drove through the countryside. There had been too much time to think about Key West and Elena, and how out of place he knew he would feel in the new surroundings. He hadn't seen his sister since he walked out on his family and left Zephyrhills more than a decade ago.

Carl Tanzler's sister came out of the house when she saw the dust from the three large trucks coming up the dirt road to her house. His last letter had said he would be arriving about this time, but she hadn't realized how much her brother was bringing with him. What in the world was that sticking out of the back of that truck? It looked like the tail of an airplane! Good Lord, where was she going to put all that stuff which he and the men started unpacking almost immediately? The tired drivers were ready to clean up and get some sleep in the boarding house downtown.

After dinner, she and the Count talked for a while over some hot tea before he fell asleep exhausted from the trip.

At this point, his sister was wondering whether his return was such a good idea after all. Carl didn't seem like the same Carl to whom she had bid farewell thirteen years before. Naturally, he was older, so was she; but it was the obsessive look in his eyes which was the most different. And he talked about subjects on which she would rather not hear, like his lovely bride Elena. Everyone in Zephyrhills, including her, had read about Carl and the dead girl. This very morning, they were reading the newspaper account of the dynamite explosion at the tomb. Word quickly spread that he was in town, and that he'd brought a wingless airplane with him.

Actually, his sister was as horrified as everyone else by what he had done and his notoriety. She knew his wife well, and she wasn't any Spanish girl called Elena Hoyos who had died in 1931 in Key West. Her sister-in-law was Mrs. Doris Tanzler, who lived just down the road.

The words his sister most wanted to hear from Carl after he'd been there a few days were, "Is there anything I can do to help?" but Carl never uttered them because he couldn't be distracted from his work. There was still so much for him to do for his dead sweetheart. He must tell their story, write a book, and paint watercolors telling about his immortal, transcendental love.

After his things were organized and he was settled in, the Count tried writing his memoirs inside his sister's house. It proved to be impossible. Von Cosel wasn't used to living with the living. The loud opening and closing of doors, everyday tasks, coupled with his sister's occasional fits of epilepsy, distracted him. He needed a place where he could concentrate.

So, it was only natural that he took refuge in:

Cts Elaine von Cosel C-3

—his airship with the huge wheels that he still fantasized would someday, upon completion, allow him to triumphantly land on the water of the Key West harbor and taxi up to the dock—the hero returning home. It didn't bother the Count that he hadn't flown in a plane since he learned to fly from Monsieur Geau in Australia in 1912 (if the Count had really been there that year). He still considered himself an aviator.

Meanwhile the war in Europe was heating up and by 1942, the United States was in the thick of it. Suspicious-looking German natives living within American borders, including Mr. Tanzler, were put under surveillance to make sure they weren't spies transmitting vital information to the enemy. It's always better to err on the side of caution, was the approach taken by the internal security forces of the United States in Carl Tanzler's case. When the officials arrived in Zephyrhills, they probably didn't know what to think of the potential traitor they had been assigned to observe—airplane and all. No telling what was reported back to headquarters, but somewhere down the chain-of-command, a decision was reached. Just to be sure it wasn't a trick plane that just looked like it couldn't fly, they told Carl Tanzler von Cosel to take the wheels off of the wingless fuselage.

Without the absurdly big wheels, the plane sat at an angle that made the seat in the cabin uncomfortable—yet it was there, in the little cockpit he had shared with Elena, that the intrepid author took pen in hand and, in the midst of all his adversity, began to write his troubled story:

> So in the cabin of Elena's airship, where her coffin had rested so long ago, I sat down and wrote this account. My position was cramped in the pilot seat and made all the more uncomfortable; war regulations made it necessary to remove the wheels from the plane so that my quarters were not only extremely narrow, but slanting backward. I am no professional writer; I am not a poet; but I have a little gift of painting, and so I have tried to express in pictures what I could not say in words. In this manner, happiness of a kind came back to me; my life again has a purpose; although it is sad that

these pictures (seen by visitors at my place) cannot be reproduced in this magazine.

Admittedly, my experiments in resurrecting Elena were partially successful. Too often my work was interrupted and disturbed by outside circumstances beyond my control. But I am not giving up. I feel that the invaluable experience already gained lends itself as a reassurance that new experiences could be crowned with success. Elena's body, true enough, is now interred, but her dying wish that she and I should live together has been granted to both of us. She is with me as I write this, she advises me; in fact, it is her hand which, I feel, is leading my pen.

So then, I wish to thank, through this account, all those thousands of kindhearted and big hearted friends who have come to my support in my hour of need. It was their faith in me which has restored me to new life; it is to them I dedicate this book, and to my Elena, as she was the first who visited me while in jail.

Carl Tanzler's life in Zephyrhills was not nearly as flamboyant as his last years in Key West. In a way, he liked the return to the first peacefulness he had known since living alone on Rest Beach and then Flagler Street. Of course, he missed his bride, fisherman Frank, the dogs, and the ocean.

Still, he was a celebrity, and there were more than a few who wanted to meet the man who kept a corpse he called his wife. This was especially true since the townsfolk knew of Doris Tanzler, his live wife. What kind of person, they asked themselves, immersed in their everyday life, would exchange the warmth and affection between live husbands and wives for the cold embrace of death? Everyone wanted to know the answer, including his bewildered spouse and her equally bewildered daughter, who had been sheltered from the truth as much as possible. Eventually, those who wanted to see for themselves badly enough, came up with an excuse to go over to Carl's sister's place.

It wasn't long before Doris saw the strange, wingless aircraft, its proposed pilot and the myriad of inventions lying around in various stages of completion.

Interestingly, it was Mrs. Doris Tanzler who, once again, showed compassion for her ex-husband. It never occurred to him that he was the one who was mean-spirited, callous, unfaithful, and non-supportive.

Doris took the initiative and called on Carl at his sister's, and she eventually took him to the place where his daughter Crystal was buried. Looking down at the tiny grave, she cried softly as he quietly looked down, for the first time, at their child's burial place.

Now that he had finished writing his memoirs, he had time to make a monument for little Crystal the way he had made one for his Elena. At the head of a cement slab he had poured and smoothed, he made an arch with a cross that stood about three feet off the ground. Under the arch was a headstone that read simply:

**CRYSTAL TANZLER
OUR DARLING**

There was no date of birth or death. At the foot of the cement slab, he placed one of his handmade cement urns, like the ones on Elena's mausoleum, where flowers could be placed or planted. Though he was belatedly expressing some grief over the death of his daughter, most of his thoughts were focused on getting the memoirs of his undying love for Elena Hoyos published.

After all of the work he had put into writing the memoirs, looking for a publisher was a frustrating endeavor. Letters had to be written and chapters sent off to publishers who might be interested in his chronicle.

> *Zephyrhills, Florida, R.D.*
> *July 15—43*
> *[To whom the letter was written has been blacked out.]*
> *Hoping this will find you well in Key West, as it left me also well here in Zephyrhills. Since the last two years, I am here on this farmland two miles away from town all to myself like a hermit writing the book, finishing it with all illustrations.*
>
> *The book of Elena is finished and the manuscript ready to go in print at last. It was quite a job, I assure you, as I had to work here under great difficulties owing to the war situation and other setbacks.*
>
> *I guess you have been wondering where I got to, but the pa-*

pers had been publishing where I went. That time it was a hurry-up job, because Porter wanted his shed, so I had to leave many things behind. And I had to get somewhere to be left alone, undisturbed for my writings.

But, alas, it proved otherwise to my great disappointment. I found I was very much disturbed in my work by thymiles [?] of my sister here who is suffering from epilepsy.—So I had to retreat into my airship to be left undisturbed with all my papers, as nothing was safe from her interference, except the airship where Elena's body had been laying so long.

As there is no such thing as a publisher for thousands of miles around I had to find one way up north in Massachusetts. He is willing to undertake it and handle the whole business under contract and has approved and OKed the manuscript.

Now our old contract has expired last year and Thereton from Miami is out for good. His picture story was no good anyhow, being made up on the presumption I was dead or would be disposed of.

Here is a real chance that we both can become rich after all if we work together. This story written by myself is complete in every detail, including your part played in it. It is titled:

"The Secret of the Tomb." It comprises seventy thousand words and seventy pictures in color and black and white. And is a biographic record and the same time a romantic love story. Also recording scientific physical and metaphysical phenomena.

The publishing firm is of reliable good standing and has examined the manuscript, found it of extraordinary interest and has accepted it for printing and publishing under contract. In which I receive 33 1/3 percent of all sales of the book and 75 percent of the undertakings from all moving pictures or other stage plays on this subject. I think this is fair, don't you?

Now also they want a cash deposit of $2,000 to cover expenses for outlays on plates engravings and printing of the first edition only. There is no charge for all further prints or editions. The contracts will be then signed and work begins right away.

As my sister has no more money but her land and I also had to spend mine to assist her in her affliction—I had to call my distant relations in the north only to find they had died in the meantime.—It is possible that you could locate someone who can write out that deposit check for the publisher so we can go ahead and have that contract signed as a loan. It should be easy I think. Here in this forgotten location are just country farmers, nobody has any money, nor interest in anything but chickens, cows, and hogs.

As I am unable to get any transfer of money from my bank in Germany during the war—I have to see that someone will loan it for that purpose. But if it is possible for you to arrange this, then I will share with you in all taking.

Hoping you and your family are well and all of Key Wester Too,

I am yours truly,
G. Carl Tanzler von Cosel

The letter may possibly have been written to one of the two who posted his bail—Zorsky or Benny. Von Cosel was desperate.

The only way to ease the pain of waiting to set the record straight was to utilize his small gift for painting.

Watercolors were his medium and, rather than creating representations of a tortured and misunderstood soul, his work was calm and serene, Carl Tanzler von Cosel was at peace with himself and confident that the world would appreciate him someday. That would be the ultimate vindication.

He painted pictures of his and Elena's great escape from the Key West Cemetery, their special Christmas of 1936, and her ultimate resurrection. Included in the collection that was to accompany the manuscript were sketches of his laboratory on Rest Beach, and the electrical invention he used to treat Elena. He painted a picture of the honeymoon couple flying to heaven, and there were numerous portraits of his beloved attempting to show her unearthly beauty.

There wasn't much else for him to do. He refused to take a job that was below his dignity, and no hospital was going to hire him as an X-ray technician now that the story of his bizarre love affair with his "afterlife" bride was public information.

Chapter Nineteen

In Sickness and in Health

Much to von Cosel's chagrin, the money to publish the memoirs was never sent from the mystery person or persons in Key West to whom he'd sent his plea.

However, things did improve a little. Sometime in 1944, von Cosel moved from his sister's house to a place of his own, a rural residence in Pasco County, Florida. The move allowed him to erect a suitable indoor shrine to his beloved Elena, something his sister wouldn't allow in her home.

On a long table inside his crude little house, he put Elena's casket, and inside the casket, he placed one of his plaster of Paris death masks atop a remake of Elena's body. On the open lid of the coffin, he placed pictures of her when she was alive and hung important memorabilia. From the wall, Elena's rosary and a crucifix looked down upon her re-created form. Von Cosel was once again living alone with his bride—free to work on his plane, invent new things, and study phenomena of the universe through his microscope which he kept on the table next to his Elena.

That same year, 1944, in Key West, both Mario and Florinda (Nana) Medina died. Mario was electrocuted on February 12, trying to rescue a fellow worker when the crane he was operating hit a power line. Nana, who had been ill for some time, succumbed on April 23, age forty, to the same deadly disease that had hastily consumed her sister Elena. With Nana's passing, the entire Hoyos family had been wiped out by tuberculosis.

Though it was thought by some in Zephyrhills that the Count sold some of his aeronautical innovations to Boeing Aircraft during the war, the archivist at company headquarters in Seattle, Washington, couldn't come up with any correspondence from the iconoclastic inventor. It's entirely possible his mail was intercepted because his correspondence was certainly of interest to the government officials, who, for security reasons, were still keeping track of Carl Tanzler.

They observed von Cosel whenever he was in town and dutifully wrote down the names of those he talked to about Elena that day. The audiences he managed to corner usually looked at the ground and shook their heads uncomfortably. One Zephyrhills local recalled, "You know, he used to take people over to his house and show them the replica he had made of that girl. He always dressed up and looked neat walking around town."

Local residents felt sorry for Carl Tanzler, but they really felt sorry for his wife, who, through no fault of her own, was a marked woman as was their daughter. No longer were they simply neighbors; they were known around town as the wife and daughter of you-know-who, who did you-know-what to that Cuban girl in Key West.

Likewise, there were distant relatives of the Hoyos family who felt embarrassed and shamed that a relative of theirs had been involved in such a bizarre plot, even though much of it occurred after she had died. To this day, some Cubans who are related to or knew the Hoyos family refuse to talk about the episode. They, along with the Tanzlers, wish the whole thing would just go away.

Von Cosel finally found a publisher for his memoirs a little over a year after World War II ended in 1945. With the Third Reich in ashes, the general public was inclined to forgive German nationals who spent the wartime on the side of the United States. After the armistice, von Cosel's story once again stirred interest as Americans tried to forget what they had been through collectively and sought entertainment.

Fantastic Adventures, a pulp publication, agreed to print "The Secret of Elena's Tomb." In von Cosel's letter requesting money, he said the manuscript was 70,000 words, including illustrations. Only about 37,500 words, and none of von Cosel's illustrations, were in the pared down version.

It was upsetting to the Count that his illustrations wouldn't be used, but it was the best deal he could get. At least some revenue would be coming in. Why the publisher didn't use his paintings and photographs is not known. The few surviving landscapes painted by "von Tanzler," the name many were calling him in Zephyrhills, showed that he did have some skill as an artist. At any rate, the il-lustrations used in *Fantastic Adventures* were done by Henry Sharp, who clearly had no idea what the participants looked like. Elena didn't look like herself, the Count didn't look like himself, nor do the pictures accompanying the article accurately portray the cemetery and the great escape von Cosel so hauntingly described.

On September 5, 1947, the quirky pulp publication hit the news-stands, and once again, the Count was in the limelight while Mrs. Tanzler was horrified. Beyond hurt at this point, she was thankful Carl Tanzler had left her and their daughters out of the memoirs. Still, it was one more thing she would have to live down and one more thing she would have to shield her daughter from, if possible.

The publication of his memoirs was the next to the last chapter of von Cosel's "Ulysses" Odyssey. When the money earned from the sale of his story was gone, the Count was again destitute. He couldn't even buy food. He was now old, and there really weren't any ways to earn money that were acceptable to the Count. It was during this final period of Georg Karl Tanzler's life that Doris Tan-zler showed what an exceptionally kind and compassionate woman she was.

Mrs. Tanzler and Mr. Tanzler met each week at the same park bench. Sitting on opposite ends, they would talk for a while and then she would give him two dollars and fifty cents from her fifteen-dollars-a-week salary. It wasn't much, but it allowed him to buy sar-dines and a few staples, which kept him from starving to death.

Whatever his motive, in 1950, Carl received his certificate of United States citizenship—with a peculiar addendum. Typed on the back of his citizenship papers was notification of a name change. Over seventy now, the Count wanted to change his name from Karl Tanzler to Carl Tanzler von Cosel.

Two years later, after days of not seeing von Tanzler's thin sil-houette walking erectly as he searched for wild flowers for his bride, nearby neighbors checked his home only to find unopened mail on his front porch and darkness behind closed doors. They called the sheriff who found the Count's badly decomposed body lying on the floor next to the table with the casket. The flowers in the vase by the plaster death mask had completely dried, and the petals had fallen onto the table.

The date of death on the certificate was: (month) July, (day) unknown, (year) 1952. It was the same year Dwight Eisenhower was elected president of the United States succeeding Harry Truman, who, with his wife Bess, spent their vacations in Key West. So acrimonious were the old and the new presidents' feelings toward each other that, when Eisenhower came to Key West to recuperate from a heart attack, he refused to stay in the Little White House where Truman had slept.

On August 14, with little fanfare, the son of Karl Tanzler and Pauline Schulz was buried in the Zephyrhills Cemetery near his daughter, Crystal.

His wife, his surviving daughter, and a sprinkling of friends most likely attended the burial which probably was paid for by Mrs. Tanzler. Though a newspaper account said she was unable to attend because she was a nurse in Huntington Woods, Michigan, the more likely scenario was that she was there to see him lowered into the ground.

A nameless, cement cross was set in the loose soil above his remains. At his feet lay his young daughter who died in 1934. Later, eternally resting by his side would be his wife. She, who suffered the terrible indignities that were the result of his obsessive love for Elena Hoyos, finally found peace in 1977. Decorating the graves are scarlet artificial flowers.

The death certificate failed to acknowledge his attempted name change. Officially, the deceased was listed as "Carl Tanzler, Trial [Electrical] therapist." On the certificate under "kind of business or industry," the handwritten response was, "Doctor's offices, etc." He was said to be "married" and his age was given as "72." Although since his birth date was January 12, 1877, he was seventy-six.

Responding to a letter from the honorable Earl Adams of Key West, Coleman and Furgeson, the morticians, said it was their assumption that Dr. Carl Tanzler and Count Carl von Cosel were one and the same person.

The *Key West Citizen,* Friday, August 15, 1952:

**WAX REPLICA OF ELENA MESA FOUND
IN VON COSEL'S HOME**
DID EVERYTHING HE COULD TO KEEP LOVE FOR
BEAUTIFUL GIRL ALIVE
ZEPHRYHILLS (AP)—A romantic old man who believed

his love for a young woman was stronger than death itself lay in a simple grave today near a life-sized replica of the girl.

Dead at 72, Karl Tanzler, who liked to be called Dr. Carl von Cosel, did everything he could to keep alive his love for the beautiful Elena Mesa.

Officers searching the cluttered little house where the old German X-ray technician was found dead Wednesday discovered a wax replica of Elena's body and a wax image of her head.

Both were skillfully made and the features were faithful reproductions of pictures of the girl found in albums bearing such titles as "The Secret of the Tomb" and "Elena in the Battle of Life."

Not far from the house, a handful of neighbors watched Thursday while Tanzler was buried beside his daughter Crystal....

The bearded, white-haired old man took with him to the grave the secret of what really happened to Elena's body.

Tanzler fell in love with the girl (years ago) while working in a hospital at Key West. When she died of tuberculosis, he obtained permission from her family to build a vault for her in the city cemetery.

Eight years later, in 1940, the body was found in Tanzler's shack dressed in a flimsy negligee, adorned with jewels, resting in a canopied bed. There were fresh flowers in her hair.

Tanzler told deputies he serenaded her nightly with a pipe organ he constructed and planned to fly away with her in an airplane he was building when she returned to life.

The nearly disintegrated parts of the airplane still lie in the yard of his home.

Von Cosel never finished the airplane that metaphorically defined von Cosel himself. He never made a triumphant flight back to Key West where his beloved Elena was buried. He may have daydreamed of stepping down from the cockpit of the plane named after Elena at the Key West airstrip. The crowd that would have gathered just for this occasion would applaud as he took off his avi-

ator goggles and removed his leather aviator cap—looking very
much like a returning hero.

This was never to be.

But perhaps he was at peace at last, for as he himself had said:

> Yet Divine happiness is flowing through me. For she is
> with me. Nobody could take her away from me for God
> Almighty has united our souls. She has survived death, for-
> ever and ever she is with me.
>
> And every look at her picture and every thought in my
> mind is a silent prayer of thanks to the Creator who led me
> to find her. Thanks that He gave me the strength and the
> knowledge to prolong her brief life on earth for nearly two
> years, to make it tolerable in its pains and to salvage her
> beauty from the ravages of the grave.
>
> She is my everlasting joy … God bless her.
>
> Ex tenebris lucem.

"Ex tenebris lucem,"—out of darkness comes light. Those were
the final three words of von Cosel's memoirs.

Chapter Twenty

The Story that Wouldn't Die

Through the years that followed, grocery store tabloids, detective magazines, and newspapers periodically revived snippets of the "bizarre" tale. The titles of the articles about Count Carl von Cosel and his bride were sensational, and the content of the articles what you would expect. All but a few described how Elena Hoyos died on Halloween night. Even though that isn't when it happened, it added drama.

But it was the *Tropic Magazine* article by John Dorschner that appeared on Sunday, March 5, 1972, twenty years after von Cosel's death and thirty-two years after his hearing and sanity evaluation, that confirmed medically what had all along been whispered.

The author of the article interviewed Dr. DePoo, who belatedly told what he had found during the autopsy. "The breasts really felt real. In the vaginal area, I found a tube wide enough to permit sexual intercourse. At the bottom of the tube was cotton, and in an examination of the cotton, I found there was sperm. Then I knew we were dealing with a sexual pervert."

Perhaps Dr. DePoo would have been forced to disclose the results of the autopsy had von Cosel been brought to trial, but he never was, and the doctor didn't volunteer the information. Had the doctor revealed what he knew to the packed courtroom, reporters would have been pushing and shoving their way out of the courtroom doors to break the inside story.

Following the *Tropic* article, there was a medical treatise, *The Romantic Necrophiliac of Key West,* written by Dr. Foraker. He confirmed that none of the newspaper accounts at the time of the hearing gave the necrophiliac details. Perhaps the final paragraph of Dr. Foraker's article explains why the two doctors kept von Cosel's secret for as long as they did:

In 1971, while preparing an article on the U.S. Marine Hospital, Key West, I planned to include a short section on the von Cosel case with the basic facts but disguised names. As a middle-aged 'square' I had not realized how much the times had changed until my attention was drawn to Dorschner's article in the public press, complete with true names, pictures, necrophiliac, and anatomical facts, however sordid.

Simply put, people didn't talk about things like that in print in 1940. The doctors kept their mouths shut to protect the public and the families of those involved. What von Cosel had done was best left undisclosed.

However, there is no doubt as to what Dr. Foraker observed.

I attended this autopsy on the desiccated corpse which had a reconstructed face, breasts, arms, legs, trunk, and a vaginal tube constructed so that intercourse could be simulated.

He played the organ for her, emphasizing Wagner, and felt she could hear the music. He continued working on the airplane, alleging that when finished, "it would carry them both high into the stratosphere, so that radiation from outer space could penetrate Elena's tissues and restore life to her somnolent form."

Did von Cosel really believe all those things he had said and written? He was eccentric, no doubt, but did he promulgate some of those weird beliefs as a cover for necrophilia?

Dr. Foraker answered those rhetorical questions by first discussing the medical uniqueness of the case. Then he psychologically profiled the Count by paralleling his behavior with the notions of 1800's German Romanticism.

A search of the available psychiatric and forensic medical literature has revealed no duplicate of the von Cosel case. Most references, such as Kraft-Ebing, discuss necrophilia involving recently deceased female corpses.

Dr. Foraker then quoted two pertinent opinions concerning this case:

> I have searched the forty to fifty years of accumulation of literature in sex crimes and related problems and have found no case as yet similar to this one.
> —William G. Eckert, M.D., editor INFORM, International Reference Organization in Forensic Medicine and Sciences

> "This is by far the most bizarre case of necrophilia I have come across."
> —Joseph C. Rupp, M.D., Ph.D., Medical Examiner, Corpus Christi, Texas

Dr. Foraker went on to discuss what effects the German Romantic movement may have had on von Cosel's thoughts.

> Certainly von Cosel had a solid German education which exposed him to "Romanticism." The romantic movement in German Romanticism is heavily concerned with death. This background may have been involved in his thoughts and actions in this case....
> Wagner's conception of love in death concludes most of his operas: The highest love cannot survive on earth, so the ultimate expression is for the living to commit suicide in order to join the departed....
> D.G. Rossetti, the poet, saw an afterlife filled with sensual lust ("The Blessed Damozel") and in his own life dwelt in the grave with his wife ("The House of Life"), whom he exhumed to retrieve his poetry which was buried with her. Edgar Allan Poe saw the highest of all possible topics for the poem as the love of a man for a dead woman....

Next he wrote of the translation of poetic notion to actual behavior.

> Praz spoke of Romantic Necrophilia as distant from other necrophilia and assumed it was more self-conscious.

He suggested that the Romantic "fascination of a beautiful woman already dead" was influenced by the vampire legend....

A striking example of necrophilia in American literature is Faulkner's "A Rose for Emily." In it, one of his classic Southern spinsters fed arsenic to a reluctant suitor, then kept his unembalmed body in a bed in a locked room for forty years. Ending his story with the cryptic comment, "The body had apparently once laid in the attitude of an embrace."

Dr. Foraker made a critical mistake in his analysis near the end of the article when he incorrectly stated the song "Boda Negra" (Black Wedding) was inspired by von Cosel and Elena. It was exactly the other way around. There is no doubt whatsoever that it was written by a Colombian Romanticist before Elena's death, but this fact emphatically reinforces the doctor's hypothesis—that von Cosel was heavily influenced by other great romantic notions. Von Cosel's life was imitating heavenly inspired art.

How different would the public's reaction toward the Count have been had the doctors told on von Cosel? Probably not much. In truth, in the small-town, close atmosphere of Key West in the 1930s and 1940s, everyone probably knew.

Blame it on the Tropics

After Carl von Cosel died, the dilapidated airplane he never fin-ished was moved into a neighbor's yard as a toy for the chil-dren to play on. It was a strange finale to an even stranger story. The airship didn't even look as though it was made of metal. Prob-ably constructed of canvas and wood, its sides looked more like the sides of an old boat that had been patched than a plane. Eventually, it rotted in its backyard cemetery while von Cosel did the same un-derground.

In Key West, Elena's mausoleum was left almost as it was after the explosion until von Cosel died in 1952. Nobody paid much at-tention to it as the palm trees and weeds grew up around the cement vault with the door blown off its hinges by dynamite.

Because von Cosel never relinquished ownership of the plot, it was sold, in all likelihood, to its present and future occupants when his estate was settled.

The tale which titillated a nation is still fascinating. The Count was a sometimes charming, sometimes irritating character who, at the same time, was an unabashed romantic. No matter how seri-ously he took himself, he did some things that were hilarious whether he knew it or not. To be frank, I've laughed when I shouldn't have, but there is something about the whole affair that is amusing as well as grotesque and poignant, often at the same time. Laughter becomes the only release from the dramatic, even tragic, tension.

The time frame and location add to the mystic nature of his foibles. There is something about Cayo Hueso and its inhabitants that seems to promote intriguing behavior. Key West author, Vaughn Gibson—an excellent writer and observer of human na-ture—believed the perception of the "laid back in paradise" was a myth. He likened the atmosphere of Key West to living in a pressure cooker. There seems to be a creative force hovering over the island that drives people in the tropical climate. Blame it on the tropics, then. Carl Tanzler never would have committed such acts in Dresden, Saxony, Germany, nor would he have behaved the way he did in Zephyrhills with his family surrounding him.

Count von Cosel adapted well to life in Key West—he was both driven and creative.

In recounting this story, I had to, in certain instances, make some assumptions and fill in some of the blanks. Obviously, I couldn't know exactly what Elena had on her mind as she sat in front of Dr. von Cosel's X-ray machine. Absent a court transcript, there is no way of reproducing exactly what was said at the hearing. But I have always tried to stay within my self-imposed zone of truth while resurrecting the characters. It's likely that Elena had the thoughts I described at some point in time. The courtroom dialogue was a composite of newspaper accounts, the memoirs, and quotes from people in attendance—not verbatim but true to the flavor of the circus-like atmosphere.

As for the unsolved conflicts and mysteries, I presented the possibilities as best I could, and even sometimes hinted at what I suspected was the truth.

Count von Cosel's written account of what he did and why he did it added a completely new dimension to my story of his life. On the surface, it was wrong to take a dead girl from her grave, mummify her, and love her. Why then was the sentiment at the time so overwhelmingly in the Count's favor? It was the paradoxical nature of this cocksure German immigrant and his morbid love that made this story so incredible. The length of time he kept Elena, the attention he gave her, and the obvious affection he felt for her mitigated the hard cold facts. In this book I have tried to bring out not only these facts but to examine and portray these aspects of character and motivation which enrich the story.

Re-creating the flavor of Key West is something I hope I've done well enough. Unlike the rest of the country and much of the world, the Keys had a much easier time during the Depression. In fact, the thirties, I've been convinced, was a very special time to be living here.

Yes, there were mosquitoes and water was pumped by hand from wells and cisterns; few had phones, and air conditioning was decades away, but not a single person to whom I talked regretted where they were and the life they led. It seems the locals enjoyed themselves.

Finding out about the song "La Boda Negra" and then listening to the beautiful melody was one of the more exciting moments in my efforts to peel back the layers of the characters and events. I couldn't help but wonder what kind of person was the composer, Alberto Villalon?

What kind of person would write such a song about digging up dead lovers? It's doubtful he made the story up. In all probability, the song is about something that actually happened. While wondering about the author of "The Black Wedding," it dawned on me that I had done the same thing when I wrote the ballad of "Maria Elena Hoyos and Count Carl von Cosel."

The two big influences on Key West at the time, wrecking and the cigar making—were a fitting backdrop for the romance of the decade, perhaps the century. I walked into the moving van warehouse that once was a cigar factory and thought of Elena's father, who was part of that industry. They were still using the wooden elevator made by the "Morse Elevator Company" that took the raw tobacco to the second and third floors and brought the finished cigars down to street level. Close by Glynn Archer Elementary School, where the W.P.A. murals were painted, is another building that was once a large cigar factory. With the windows bricked over, they look like warehouses, but originally they were three-story brick buildings with large arched windows to let in the breeze, and high ceilings to give the heat a place to go.

I've had a lot of interesting and often amusing experiences following the Count's cold trail: viewing the memorabilia, reading the literature, walking the same streets, and seeing many still extant sights. Perhaps most humorous of all have been some of my conversations with those who are knowledgeable or were there. Lynda Hambright at the Monroe County Library has a twinkle in her eye when she kiddingly offers her insight: "If Elena hadn't taken the gold, none of this would have happened to her." I agree, and she shouldn't have translated the song, "La Boda Negra," for him, either.

On her head he placed a wreath of flowers
Full of love he held her close to him

He closed his eyes as he gently kissed her
Never again would he awaken

Al esqueleto regido abrazado—her rigid skeleton he embraced—
in Cayo Hueso, the Island of Bones.

BEN HARRISON, APRIL 1996